TICKLED SOUL

The Philosophical Journey
of a
Doctor Turned
Middle School Teacher

BY KEITH POCHICK, MD

This book is a work of nonfiction. Some names and identifying details of people described in this book have been altered to protect their privacy.

ISBN: 978-1-966343-46-2 (hard cover)
       978-1-966343-47-9 (soft cover)
Pochick. Keith
Edited by: Amy Klein

Warren publishing
Warren Publishing
Charlotte, NC
www.warrenpublishing.net
Printed in the United States

For my wife, Meredith,
whose unshakeable groundedness allows me to
wander (and wonder) around with my head in the clouds.

For my sisters, Kristi and Kathy,
two incredible moms whose infectious joy and ceaseless quests
for creative recipe tweaks make me feel like a pampered
foreign dignitary every time I visit them.

For my daughters, Taylor and Kaycie,
whose kindness, work ethic,
and sense of humor enrich my life in ways
I never could have imagined.

Foreword

As a fellow middle school teacher and a close friend of Keith, I've had the privilege of witnessing his journey both inside and outside the classroom. Our daily chats and hearty laughs about good food, old movies, and silly videos, along with our profound discussions about life and the challenges of teaching, have given me a unique perspective on the valuable insights he shares in this book.

Keith's transition from practicing clinical medicine to teaching middle school science is a testament to his boundless curiosity and optimism. His ability to draw from a lifetime of experiences and distill them into meaningful reflections is truly inspiring. This book, which he describes as a "missive" or "philosophical musing," is a culmination of his thoughts, shaped by years of interpreting and synthesizing life's complexities. In these pages, Keith explores fundamental concepts such as life, love, eternal life, free will, purpose, motivation, and what he calls the "soul tickle." His unique perspective, shaped by his medical background and teaching experiences, offers readers a fresh and thought-provoking take on these timeless topics.

This book is not just a collection of thoughts; it is a legacy, a gift from the author to his children, to future generations, and to you, the reader. As you read this book, I hope you find the same inspiration and joy that I have found in Keith's words. His reflections are not only a testament to his wisdom and compassion but also a call to action for all of us to live meaningful and purposeful lives. May you find inspiration in his reflections and be encouraged to approach life with a renewed sense of purpose and fulfillment. Enjoy the journey.

Ann Parker

Middle School Math Faculty, Providence Day School

Prologue

This book took somewhere between two weeks and forty-eight years for me to write. Akin to a brief, intense, July thunderstorm, the phase of actively transcribing a first draft of thoughts and beliefs onto pages only lasted a couple of weeks. Synthesizing and adapting those thoughts and beliefs into words took an entire lifetime; that part was more like the way dozens of variables must align over time to create storm conditions in a precise spot.

As a student, I dreaded writing assignments. To me, an essay or book report was the young person's equivalent of taxes; there was no enjoyment in it, and it was best to just get it over with and move on. In retrospect, I think that I simply hadn't lived through enough varied experiences or met enough people to enable me to create engaging stories and essays. Now that I've helped build a family, navigated a few professional challenges and changes, and developed symbiotic peer relationships, my thoughts and ideas carry more meaning and nuance.

While it isn't likely to launch ships or move mountains, this is the most ambitious writing project I've ever undertaken; the others don't even come close in length or depth. So I'm not sure whether to call this book an *essay* or a *manifesto*. It seems far too long to file under essay, but not nearly exhaustive or detailed enough to be considered a manifesto offering directions on how to live. Maybe it's a missive, a long letter to my kids and future grandkids. It could be that philosophical musing fits best, but my life story already seems too concrete to be a set of musings. Since I don't want to stray too far into semantics before the book has even begun, I'll just admit now that it probably doesn't matter what we call it.

I imagine it's best to start by exploring why my ideas and thoughts may matter to you—what have I done to earn the chance to draw your mind closer to mine? In most senses, my life is unremarkable. I'm an unlikely protagonist—the everyman character in a movie, but with twenty extra pounds and a couple of digits subtracted on the one-to-ten attractiveness scale. Yet there is one aspect of my story that students and fellow teachers find most interesting: After twenty years, I voluntarily left a career in clinical medicine to become a middle school science teacher. Most of my fellow teachers can't seem to solve that puzzle, no matter how many metaphorical vowels they buy. Why would I take such a pay cut at the peak of my earning potential? Why would I leave a setting of professional partnership and esteem to start at the ground floor in a career where the people I serve have little concern for my title or achievements? The best answer I have is that I was compelled to change. Eventually, I stopped resisting the compulsion and began to follow it; I guess some combination of curiosity, confidence, burnout, wanderlust, optimism, and naivete made the jump inevitable. Whatever it was, I'm grateful for it.

With that background, you as a reader can be assured that you're about to examine the philosophy of someone who has done a significant amount of soul-searching. It seems like the first thing every philosopher should know is their own soul. Even though I'm just an amateur, at least I've got that base covered.

Planning the sequence of chapters in this book was a painstakingly intentional process. Before I could even begin to articulate my own philosophy, I needed to define my purpose. But since purpose is vaporous without a firm identity, I had to critically examine my identity beforehand. Because identity is built on a foundation of beliefs, analyzing my formative years and experiences became the first prerequisite. So this narrative grew as I worked backward, retrospectively surveying each stage of my journey, both on the ground and in my own mind.

The spire and beacon are typically the most memorable characteristics of a skyscraper, much like each individual's thoughts and actions reveal their unique and persisting personal philosophy. The highest level of self, one's personal philosophy resembles the skyscraper's spire, supported by steel beams of purpose resting firmly upon a bedrock of beliefs. So I began writing this book by articulating the foundation of beliefs upon which I have built my sense of purpose. Then, after defining and establishing my purpose, I could explore the motivations for my thoughts and actions. In sharing my thoughts and actions with you, I hope to bring my personal philosophy to life.

All living things come into existence; all living things die. That central concept of life science has surely shaped the way I see the universe. Since I've been a life scientist for my entire career, and a student of biology for much longer than that, you'll find that my personal philosophy and current spiritual beliefs both rest on foundational biological principles. It's also best to tell you now that this writing contains at least two scoops of politics. I've never understood the policy of avoiding political and religious discussions; if those two are off the table, what's left that's worth talking about?

Seemingly unanswerable metaphysical and moral questions have dominated my thoughts for as long as I can remember. As an adolescent, staring into the mirror, I wondered how, in a sea of billions of humans, I was me and not anyone else. At times, I felt as if I were imprisoned, never having the chance to experience a life other than my own. But more often, I felt lucky that the universe afforded me an abundance of resources and opportunities that billions of people could not even imagine. Depending on the circumstances, my introspective tendency can be both a virtue and a character flaw. Today, while I still find myself unable to definitively answer many of the questions that occupy my thoughts, I remain thankful for the luxury of free time to roll them around in my independent mind and for the gift of freedom to express them to you.

What you're about to read reveals the path and state of my soul through the first forty-eight years that I've owned it. As you read, you may occasionally be struck with the desire to pause and examine your own beliefs, purpose, and motivations. I highly encourage this. How else can we begin to understand our thoughts and actions without understanding the beliefs undergirding them?

Chapter 1

LIFE

Energy is life.
You must constantly use it
till you become it.
—Me

Get up offa that thing, and dance till you feel better.
—James Brown, "Get Up Offa That Thing"

THE ONLY REASONABLE BEGINNING to a book on my own philosophy is the subject of life. I'm a biologist by education, training, and trade. Every day of my adult existence, I've read about, investigated, offered advice on, or taught the subject of life. Sit in on an entry-level biology class, and you'll find that, after the teacher has reviewed the syllabus with the students, the definition of life comes next.

Biology textbooks, scholars, and teachers define *life* in a specific, regimented way that I'll explain now. After this explanation, I'll attach to that official definition of life an addendum that has become a cornerstone of my personal philosophy. So, for this part, strap on your lab goggles if you still have them. But if science isn't your thing, don't worry. This is a necessary biology review, but it's a pretty short one. Here are the criteria that something must meet for us to call it *alive:*[1]

- **Respiration:** Since all living things are composed of cells, and the simplest living things are composed of a single cell, for our current purpose, it's best to view respiration at the cellular level. The terminology can be confusing, but it's helpful to understand that cellular respiration happens on a much smaller scale than breathing air in and out of the lungs. I'll spare you the biochemical details of cellular respiration; they're pretty boring, and I don't remember them all anyway. But in general terms, respiration means that living cells take in oxygen and combine it with fuel to create energy. With few exceptions, every cell must create its own energy in order to survive, perform its function, grow, reproduce, and repair damage. That means each of the forty trillion cells in every human has the structural and molecular machinery to turn oxygen and fuel into biochemical energy. When a cell stops respiring, it can no longer function, and it will die.
- **Growth:** Cells grow in both size and number. Yeast cells increase in size and divide to make new yeast cells. Humans and dolphins begin as single cells and grow exponentially into trillions of cells as they become adults. Just about everyone has learned (and forgotten) the stages of mitosis at least once. Reviewing them now isn't important; appreciating that new cells arise from older cells is.
- **Excretion:** In the process of growing, functioning, and making energy, living things make waste products. The mammalian examples of stool and urine are unpleasantly illustrative on a large scale, but at the cellular level, respiration produces carbon dioxide (CO_2) gas. This CO_2 is toxic to animal cells; if they don't expel it, they will die.
- **Reproduction:** Living things pass along genes through DNA, and living offspring inherit these genes. Life can perpetuate life. Before a human ever exists on its own, genes have already determined thousands of characteristics, some immediately visible and others tightly hidden. Notably, nature occasionally violates this rule of

reproduction: Pretty much everyone agrees that a mule is alive, but mules are sterile and cannot reproduce.[2]

- **Metabolic activity:** Human cells make thousands of different proteins called enzymes[3] that enable them to grow, produce energy, and function properly. Instead of each of your forty trillion cells making every single enzyme, your cells become specialized into many different types. Within a relatively small organ like your pancreas, specialized cells make enzymes to digest proteins, carbohydrates, and fats, each in a highly targeted way. In addition, your pancreas produces two classes of hormones to regulate blood sugar. Your pancreas is just one piece of a complex metabolic machine known as the digestive system. A healthy digestive system takes in an incredible array of foods, breaks them up into microscopic bits, and absorbs the useful stuff into the bloodstream. From there, the nutrients can travel to the rest of the body's tissues and become the raw materials for each metabolically active cell to create energy.

- **Movement:** Swimming fish and flying birds are perfect illustrations of life's movement. Most scientists, however, make a valid argument that movement is not required to meet the definition of life. An oak tree doesn't move without the wind; neither does a mushroom on the forest floor. Despite this lack of motion, pretty much every scientist classifies plants and fungi as living. A sunflower slowly turning to align with the sun throughout the course of the day and a Venus flytrap snapping shut when triggered provide a bit of wiggle room for the argument that plants do, in fact, move. But as with the case of the mule above, our human desire to file everything into perfectly neat categories often fails us.

- **Response to stimuli:** Accidentally touch a hot stove, and your hand instantly jerks away. This motion happens before the sensation of pain even registers in the brain. Sensory neurons in the fingertips detect potentially dangerous heat, and the impulse immediately travels to your spinal cord, much like electric charge traveling through a wire. Within the spinal cord, a motor (movement) nerve receives the impulse and quickly relays it to your bicep muscle. Your bicep contracts, removing your hand from the heat. In humans and other complex mammals, this entire process of immediately sensing danger and preventing tissue damage plays out in about 1/100 of a second.[4]

Turning our attention to less-advanced organisms, we find that, surprisingly, many living things without spinal cords, muscles, or even nerves respond effectively to stimuli. The heliotropism of the sunflower described above is a simple, elegant example of a stimulus response. Even paramecia, single-celled living organisms categorized as protists, will "put it in reverse" and back away from unfavorable stimuli, such as suboptimal temperatures or toxins, then begin swimming forward in a different direction.[5]

Now that we've covered the classic biological criteria for life, I'd like to invite in a physics term and give you another criterion to consider: *Living things oppose inertia.* In physics, inertia is "the property of matter by which it continues in its existing state of rest unless that state is changed by an external force."[6] All living cells are incessantly moving matter around. They pull in and push out molecules and ions on a microscopic level; they collaborate as tissues and organs to propel solids, liquids, and gases on a larger scale. Recall from our above discussion on respiration that living cells must convert fuel and oxygen into usable energy; in the incessant battle against inertia, energy is the only weapon living things have in their arsenals. The instant an organism stops using energy, its individual battle against inertia is over.

Let's consider a specific example from cell biology. Animal cells have a set of membrane proteins called sodium-potassium exchange pumps. Each pump does exactly what its name suggests: takes three positively charged sodium ions and pumps them outside the cell and, in doing so, brings two positively charged potassium ions into the cell. Why does this matter? Since three positive charges leave the cell every time the pump operates, while only two positive charges enter, the cell becomes polarized:

The inside of the cell is negatively charged, while the outside is positively charged. This creates the electric potential for the cell to depolarize, returning to its neutral state, which is the entire basis of how nerve cells, or neurons, function. Before a neuron can depolarize to generate and transmit its electrical impulse, it must first become polarized. As we said, the sodium-potassium exchange pump performs the crucial role of polarizing the neuron. The neuron must maintain this electric potential and ion differential to survive and function. What does the sodium-potassium exchange pump need in order to work? It needs energy in the form of ATP (adenosine triphosphate). ATP is the energy-containing molecule cells make when they combine oxygen and fuel through respiration. When human cells are no longer making adequate amounts of ATP, a myriad of vital processes grind to a halt, including the sodium-potassium exchanger mentioned above.

Sodium concentration inside our cells is only one of hundreds of variables that humans and other higher mammals must balance to achieve proper cell and organ function. The broad term for this balancing act is *homeostasis*, from the Greek root words for *similar* and *standing still*.[7] *Homeostasis* refers to the ways in which variables such as body temperature, water balance, and blood sugar remain stable throughout an organism's existence. However, our cells themselves do anything but stand still as they carry out the processes of homeostasis—we must constantly expend energy to maintain so many variables within specific ranges. Thousands of different hormones, enzymes, and ion pumps work in concert to keep the internal environments of our cells incredibly stable.

This concert happens without any conscious direction of our own; a primitive segment of the brain called the hypothalamus conducts everything. The hypothalamus tells our kidneys to hold on to water when we are sweating and haven't had a drink for a while; it tells our muscles to start shivering to generate heat when we are out in the cold unprepared. Yet because it is so dependable and ubiquitous, healthy people tend to take the physiological brilliance of homeostasis for granted. A patient with heart failure, on the other hand, is all too aware that their ability to maintain a proper fluid balance is severely limited. If we view the heart as a pump, it is easy to predict what happens when the pump's power is reduced—water is going to back up somewhere. In the case of heart failure, excess fluid primarily settles in the legs and lungs.

To sustain homeostasis, all living things must continuously harness energy and oppose inertia. Any being that is not actively opposing inertia is no longer living. It is dead. Its corpse may still exist in the sense that a rock exists, but it is no longer alive. In humans, the transition between life and death is called *shock*. Shock in the physiological sense is quite different than in the literary one; physiological shock is not a state of surprise or disbelief, but rather a state of inadequate oxygen and fuel delivery to the cells and tissues. When deprived of oxygen and fuel, cells lose their capacity to create energy. Without ample energy, cells can no longer oppose inertia. When cells cannot oppose inertia, the beautifully designed mechanisms of homeostasis crumble; cells, tissues, and organs cannot perform their respective functions and begin to die. In the absence of a skilled medical team to rapidly identify and correct the shock state, the entire organism will succumb to inertia shortly thereafter.

Each of the seven qualities of living things mentioned above depends upon energetic forces that oppose inertia; in turn, each of these qualities contributes mightily as individual organisms wage their wars against inertia. While it's obvious that movement opposes inertia, we should recognize that each of the other six life-defining processes do as well. When cells perform respiration, they transform reactants into different energy-containing molecular products by utilizing enzymes to break and form new bonds. Reproduction and growth are clear battles against inertia. A brand-new living thing arising from an old one is the polar opposite of death. Building obviously opposes inertia, and what is growth if not building? A single cell explosively and exponentially growing into a trillion-celled organism over the course of a few months outshines the most skilled and well-funded construction team on Earth.

This is not to suggest that everything with the capacity to oppose inertia is alive. A flowing river is not alive; neither is a battery that pushes and pulls electrons around a circuit. But I believe the converse to be absolutely true: Everything that is alive is actively opposing inertia. Each organism's life is a constant, albeit ultimately losing, battle against inertia. As I described above, death occurs when an organism has fully transitioned to an inert state of complete rest.

So, in this sense, the enemy of life is not death; the enemy of life is inertia. Most humans have the innate capacity to understand and appreciate this truth, which helps explain why sports, dance, and music have captivated us for centuries. One who is visibly opposing inertia is celebrating life. We swim because we can; we shoot hoops because we can; we hike because we can; we throw darts (or axes) because we can. Other than the very young, each of us is fully aware that one day inertia will win. But it won't be today—today we are alive. One of the many joys (and occasional frustrations) of teaching and coaching young people is the wonder of their near-constant motion. Inertia hasn't taken hold of them like it has seized us crusty old people. Every day, I get hundreds of reminders of what it was like to be young—I can't help but absorb doses of my students' infectious energy.

IN THE BROADEST SENSE, this is a story of life. My life is a single example out of billions, yet it proves that no mandate forces us to remain in unsatisfying roles or jobs for forty years. Admittedly, I'm still a work in progress, but overcoming personal and professional inertia is the most progress I've ever made in a single step.

Chapter 2

TIME

It's not enough to be industrious; so are the ants.
What are you industrious about?
—Henry David Thoreau

Because it's their time. Their time! Up there!
Down here, it's our time. It's our time down here.
—Mikey, *The Goonies*

To INTRODUCE THE CIRCULATORY system to my eighth-grade science classes, we typically start with figuring out approximately how many times a human heart beats over a lifetime. How many times does your heart beat at rest in one minute? What about in an hour? A day? A year? How many years does an average human live; how many heartbeats occur over a lifetime? Most of the students' calculations land somewhere around three billion heartbeats per lifetime. That number sounded like a lot to me until I realized that I'm already past halfway there.

At its core, time is only a reminder of our mortality; some philosophers argue that time is a human invention born out of human necessity. I was in the editing phase of this book when I learned that my concept of time converges with that of Immanuel Kant—if not for my ignorance of the famous philosophers, I'd have credited him years ago.[8] But maybe philosophy is like science in that if the same conclusion is reached by different, independent observers, the conclusion becomes more valid. Back to the subject of time—if we were immortal, why would we need time? I imagine we would still compete in races and other events, but if we were immortal, couldn't we just hold one-on-one hundred-meter footraces for all eternity? Without the constraints of aging or time, everyone could have an unlimited number of chances to prove they were the fastest. Would there really be a need to invent and measure seconds or fractions of seconds in that eternal worldwide contest when we could just line up the next runners and see who wins? We measure time because the human mind needs to measure it; the human mind needs to measure time because the human body's existence is finite and destined to eventually surrender to inertia.

As with other standards of scientific measurement, the definition of a single second has become increasingly sophisticated. Measurements based on sunlight, day length, and dividing circles into degrees and minutes have evolved into an atomic definition of the second. For modern scientists, a second is the amount of time it takes pure Cesium atoms to emit 9,172,631,770 cycles of microwave radiation.[9] I hope you weren't expecting poetry in that definition. Even though we have strict and very specific parameters for measuring time, I've come to appreciate that, like images, sounds, scents, and tastes, individuals can perceive the same segment of time quite differently.

It's been almost two years since I left clinical medicine. Twenty years on the frontlines of American healthcare brought me numerous gifts. I paid off my loans and became financially secure. I formed numerous friendships with brilliant and witty colleagues. For well over a decade, I achieved professional fulfillment by serving those in need. In a later chapter, I'll discuss the joys and thrills I experienced in gaining competence and confidence. My perception of time, however, became severely warped over the course of my twenty years in medicine. I never realized this shift happened until after I walked away and began my new career in education.

My residency training in emergency medicine was at a busy, urban, level 1 trauma center. The approachability of our attending physicians coupled with the severity of illness, volume, and diversity of our patient population drew top-tier medical-school graduates from across the country. The cultivating experience of my residency was transformative; it developed in me the skill and confidence to undertake a nearly seamless transition into a post-residency emergency medicine career. Even knowing what I know now, I wouldn't go back and change a minute of that experience. But ultimately, nothing could prepare me for how my sense of time would unravel while I was an emergency physician.

For twenty years of my professional life, I navigated a vast sea of humanity with the singular, shortsighted goal of arriving at the next case. When I left a patient's bedside, I sought out the next patient. Many times, staff and colleagues directed me to the one who needed the quickest attention and interventions. Just as often, I scanned the new arrivals on the tracking board and prioritized patients based on the perceived dangers of their presenting problems, ages, and vital signs. I soon learned that, in urban and suburban ERs, a strategy of working nonstop at 100 percent effort to quickly see all the patients in order to earn some time to rest is maddeningly futile. Seeing all the patients is impossible; the work is never completed. Sure, a new platoon of staff and clinicians eventually arrives and takes over to care for the patients, but there are always more patients who need to be seen—always. Over my two decades in medicine, mid-shift reprieves became less and less frequent; they eventually became nonexistent.

Nowhere does nature abhor a vacuum more than in an urban ER. Every time a space is vacated, someone will inevitably and nearly instantly fill it. About five years into my post-residency career, I remember hustling to see the next patient in the middle of a raucous evening shift when I chanced upon a purple-faced lady in her fifties. She was covered in vomit and actively having a seizure on a stretcher in the hallway. The rest of the staff were in other patients' rooms. "Pull someone out!" I shouted. This

ER code phrase demands the eviction of a mostly stable patient from their treatment bay to clear space for the immediate resuscitation of someone who is more desperately ill.

While I was certainly incredulous and angry the first few times our team dealt with these scenarios, I eventually made my way through the stages of grief. The denial and anger evolved into sadness and, finally, a level of acceptance. Overburdened and understaffed gradually became my normal, day-to-day work environment. Physicians, nonphysician clinical workers, and health policy experts have penned volumes on "the tragedy of the commons" that has befallen emergency medicine. They have proposed dozens of helpful suggestions, strategies, and modifications to give ERs some breathing room; some hospitals have enacted several of them. I don't intend to add to that conversation now; I merely aim to provide a former insider's reflection on how the chaotic work environment described above ruined my sense of time, injured my psyche, and threatened my relationships.

Early in my clinical career, I really liked repairing lacerations, particularly facial lacerations. Patients with injuries and cuts to their faces, as well as the parents of kids with facial injuries, arrive to the ER with understandable anxiety. After peeking into the mirror following the injury, most are worried about noticeable, or even disfiguring, scars. Seeing a relived smile on the face of an anxious patient or parent after performing a well-executed facial laceration repair is incredibly validating. But performing a meticulous repair requires some time—not an inordinate amount, but a few minutes aren't typically sufficient to bring the best cosmetic results. Within a few months of residency graduation, I realized that any satisfaction I derived from the twenty minutes spent preparing and suturing a complex facial laceration would soon be replaced by the urgency of five or six new arrivals. Often, more than one of those new arrivals needed immediate evaluation and intervention.

Subconsciously, seeing such a towering amount of illness and injury occur at a single location in twenty minutes was disorienting—incongruent with the perception of the universe I had formed in the twenty-five years before I became a doctor in the ER. In order to accommodate and adopt this new reality, my subconscious brain began to perceive five minutes spent with a patient as a half hour. If I spent twenty minutes in a single patient's room, that meant someone in shock wasn't getting the interventions they needed. Those minutes meant that a seventy-five-year-old with a leaking aortic aneurysm was languishing on the verge of catastrophe. Those twenty minutes meant that a dialysis patient with severe electrolyte disturbances was approaching cardiovascular collapse. In this new reality, I no longer enjoyed repairing complex lacerations. Just a few years in the ER had given me the worst imaginable version of FOMO (fear of missing out).

My twisted perception of time carried into my life away from work. Checkout lines, traffic, and phone conversations became anxiety-riddled misery. Almost every waking minute, I was filled with a sense that I needed to be doing something different than what I was doing at that moment. Picking up my kids after a sleepover or playdate became a quest to unceremoniously peel them away from their friends as quickly as possible. On departure day after a trip or long weekend, I prodded my family to move along and leave as early as we could. If love is patient, back then I was doing a pretty miserable job loving the people around me. Meanwhile, I brushed off my impatience as an aspect of my personality. Amazingly, I don't remember anyone around me mentioning just how impatient I had become. I wonder now if our society's obsession with completing tasks and the expectation that each of us will spread ourselves unbearably thin made my pathological impatience seem acceptable. Until I left medicine, I never considered that maybe I wasn't programmed to be impatient; I never stopped to wonder if my anxiety had other root causes besides my DNA and early upbringing.

Today, as a middle school science teacher, I work in an environment of at least 90 percent positive energy—it's challenging and unpredictable, but filled with autonomy, supportive colleagues, and gleeful personalities. Across the hall from the eighth-grade science lab are math classrooms. My friend Ashley, one of the sixth-grade math teachers, loves to jump scare unsuspecting people; every couple of months, she'll hide behind a door and scare me so badly that my legs lose their muscle tone, and I have to catch myself on a table. As you'd expect, the kids love it. Math and science teachers pop into each other's classrooms to exchange advice and witty banter multiple times every day. Since we truly like each other, we naturally model a joyful, collaborative work environment to our students. Each unscripted, affirming interaction between teachers shapes our students' understanding of a healthy professional community. In a poetically ironic sense, the times that we aren't formally teaching are when we deliver our most powerful lessons. My new work environment refashioned the dread I used to feel when driving to work into contentment and excitement; I feel like I'm exactly where I belong.

After a few months of working full-time as a middle school teacher, I noticed that my personality had changed. Perhaps *reverted* is a more accurate word. I believe my most significant form of healing is this: I've recovered a healthy, normal perception of time. When I feel as though the eighth graders in my lab have been dissecting their raw chicken wings for thirty minutes, I look at the clock, and it agrees with my perception. When I have twenty minutes to spend eating lunch before heading to lunch duty, those twenty minutes feel exactly as twenty minutes should feel. When I meet with a student who needs to make up a lab or receive some guided enrichment, I don't feel internal pressure to hurry and move to the next task. In fewer than three years, I've become a person who thinks and acts differently than the perpetually hurried doctor I previously was.

I believe that resetting my perception of time has made me a better version of myself. Now, when our family has a day together without formal obligations, I can go hours and never once look at the clock. A few years ago, I wouldn't have lasted fifteen minutes without compulsively checking the time. When I'm at home and my thirteen-year-old asks to go shoot baskets, I go shoot baskets a hell of a lot more often than I used to. I don't know the meaning of life, but I know that when I'm connecting with people and strengthening my relationships, I feel closer to finding it.

Chapter 3

LOVE

I've got that joy, joy, joy, joy down in my heart.
Where?
Down in my heart.
–George William Cooke, "I've Got the Joy"

Tears stream down your face
when you lose something you cannot replace.
–Coldplay, "Fix You"

I HAVE TAKEN DECADES TO CONSIDER, rethink, and edit my definition of love. Like every human, I'm a product of my DNA and life experiences. This is not to suggest that free will hasn't enabled me to shape my own life—I firmly believe it has. But I'll save my take on the age-old debate about free will and predestination for a later chapter; for now, let's get back to my definition of love and how my experiences have influenced my understanding.

I spent twenty years as a clinical physician. The vast majority of those years were on the front lines in busy hospital emergency departments. The work was challenging and, initially, invigorating. People got sick; usually, I could help them. People got hurt; usually, I could help them too. Helping people heal brought me fulfillment and pride but, still, I found that major, sometimes insurmountable obstacles stood in the way of feeling satisfied with my job. Frequently, I saw the worst of human emotions and conditions: hatred, pain, grief, despair, neglect, addiction, and ignorance. To make matters worse, I began my medical career in the late stage of American healthcare's gradual transition from a loosely wound system of independent hospitals and clinics into a consolidated model consisting of a couple dozen regional, corporate behemoths. That combination of factors created the wrong recipe for me as a doctor.

I'll never forget a conversation I shared with one of my fellow ER physicians during a quick breather a few hours into an overnight shift. At the time, he was a seasoned emergency physician and emergency medical services (EMS) director with over twenty years of experience; I had about six years under my belt. We were both reeling and knew clearly that neither the volume nor severity of patient illness was going to let up. Only the clock would save us.

"Craig, how have you done this for twenty-two years?" I wondered aloud.

"Well, Keith, the first thing you have to understand is that it didn't always suck like this," he immediately answered.

"But I came here for a pep talk!"

He chuckled and shook his head, then chugged the rest of his hospital-sized miniature diet soda as we marched back into the onslaught of humanity.

I guess I ultimately left emergency medicine because it became a relationship that was taking more from me than it gave. As the years wore on, each shift resulted in an inevitable wound to my psyche. Like I mentioned in the preceding chapter, the increasingly untenable rate at which illness and injury came calling meant I skipped meals and breaks, had terse interactions with others, and missed opportunities for necessary debriefings with the rest of my team. At one particularly low point about ten years into my career, my wife and I met with a profession-oriented counselor. He was a kind, disarming, gray-haired man from Louisiana who explained the common threads of burnout. Nearly always, the discouraged worker senses diminishing levels of personal control and support amid increasing job demands. This toxic trifecta of trends virtually guarantees burnout; that was exactly how I felt then.

When I began my post-residency career in the ER, throughout each shift, four nurses and a clinical support technician assisted me in my assigned nine-bed zone. I felt supported, my staff felt supported, and we worked efficiently together. Our mutual support and efficient collaboration not only shortened the time our patients spent in the ER, but also helped us form more meaningful connections with them.

A less than 3:1 patient-to-nurse ratio is unheard of in modern emergency departments—most hospital administrators would call it absurd. In the final months of my tenure as an emergency physician, I patrolled a twelve-bed zone of patients, many of whom were posted up on hallway stretchers. It wasn't uncommon to find a single patient room occupied by a family of three-to-four people, all with similar illnesses. Instead of four nurses staffing my zone, there were only two. Now, if you're asking yourself how a single nurse can care for six to eight patients in the ER, the answer is that it is impossible, regardless of the nurse's acumen. In fewer than ten years, as the demands placed on me and my staff multiplied, the sense of agency and support I felt at work plummeted.

I imagine there's an argument to be made that the relatively cushy work environment of my early clinical career spoiled me. But that more comfortable environment also showed me how much a talented group of professionals can accomplish when reasonable expectations are placed upon them; our team's work set a standard of excellence in my mind. Months of steadily increasing demands coupled with dwindling collective control and support grew our team's awareness of a painful fact: While we were capable of delivering top-quality emergency care, we were no longer empowered to do so. The inability to live up to the standards we held for ourselves was toxic; a daily sense of defeat ultimately forced each of us to choose between finding a new environment or lowering our standards. I chose to find a new environment.

In 2016, I decided to leave the ER and move to an urgent care setting. The switch felt refreshing at first; I had no overnight shifts, and the patients' illnesses and injuries were less severe. Every year, many emergency physicians make fairly seamless transitions into urgent care medicine. For most of us, the trade-off is a net positive. While the pay is a bit less, the hours are more manageable, and the greatest stressor is the number of patients rather than the severity of their illnesses. Critically ill patients don't line the hallways of urgent care clinics like they do in the ER; police and EMS don't transport combative substance abusers to urgent care centers—the ER inherits all of those cases. While it's frustrating that most urgent care centers lack diagnostic resources like comprehensive in-house labs, CT scanners, and ultrasound, patients don't have to sit in urgent care treatment rooms for two weeks while awaiting placement in psychiatric facilities. Urgent care is a pretty effective escape from the ER's incessant reminders that the United States' healthcare system is in a state of collapse. This fact alone allows clinical caregivers to extend their career longevity (if not life expectancy) by transitioning from the ER to urgent care.

The urgent care administrative role I accepted in 2018 put me in a position to help recruit, onboard, and train new clinicians in a rapidly expanding organization. Initially, the work was challenging but mostly gratifying. Then, in early 2020, the COVID pandemic struck and sent our team into uncharted waters. Suddenly, we felt that we were bearing the anxieties of the entire world. Uncertainty and fear understandably accompanied the once-in-a-century pandemic, and no terrified person prioritizes patience or respect for others. The most absurd scene I remember was from a late-summer afternoon at one of our busiest clinics in Winston-Salem. I was working with Michelle, a brilliant, witty, and driven physician assistant of Cuban descent who grew up in a West Virginia holler about an hour from my hometown. Her relatively unique background helped Michelle develop a knack for connecting with almost any patient or coworker; she worked as hard as anyone in my professional past, but was unfailingly easygoing and nonjudgmental. Anytime I looked at the work schedule and saw that I'd be working alongside Michelle, my anxiety eased. She was far more than capable; I had to work as hard as I could just to keep pace with her. Pretty often, July afternoons in North Carolina bring a brief, but powerful, thunderstorm. Sometime around six in the evening, we got one. The storm was intense enough to keep most people in their homes and cars, and with only two hours left in our shift, we'd collectively seen over a hundred patients. We welcomed the reprieve for a couple of minutes until we watched in disbelief as a family of four fought its way through the driving wind and rain from the parking lot and up to our front door. A reflective car sun shield whipped wildly over their heads as they tried in vain to use it as an umbrella. The man in the group was blind; he held his dark glasses in place with one hand and clutched a white cane with the other. His wife, mother, and young daughter helped lead him to the door. In that phase of the pandemic, when it was feasible, we did our best to evaluate potential COVID patients from their cars and limit the exposures that would occur indoors. We had our clinic phone number posted on the door so that walk-in patients could call in, tell us about their symptoms, and give registration information. If the patient was a potential COVID case, we'd don a gown, grab a bucket of supplies to take to their car, and perform the evaluation there. This family obviously hadn't seen the phone number—one of them was blind, and the other three couldn't see through the deluge of rain. Our medical assistant held open the door for them so that she could get an idea of what was going on. Considering the ferocity of the storm, we figured that someone in the group was having terrible chest pain, trouble breathing, or stroke symptoms. The wife pointed to her mother-in-law and exclaimed, "SHE NEEDS A COVID TEST!" over the wind and thunder. The patient felt fine and had no symptoms at all; she had merely been exposed to a COVID case. None of them had considered that maybe Grandma wasn't in the midst of a medical emergency and could wait for a few minutes in the car until the storm passed. For months, our shared fascination with the absurd meant that one mention of this particular pandemic tale would leave Michelle and me both howling with laughter.

Unlike most outpatient clinics, our urgent care centers were never allowed to be "full," meaning we couldn't turn anyone away. Despite the crushing volume of patients and new dangers inherent in clinical jobs, the organization held firm to its "accept all comers" policy, as if clinicians' limits and breaking points did not exist. The team of professionals that we had worked so hard to build and train started to crumble; it required an enormous amount of energy for me to win even the smallest concession to help sustain our clinical staff. One evening, the leadership team celebrated one of our most-diligent nurse practitioners, Erin, who saw seventy-six patients by herself in a single shift during a particularly brutal wave of the pandemic. I knew that the last thing Erin needed was a celebration; she needed help, or at least for someone to pump the brakes. Ultimately, I realized the futility of trying to force my values to align with those of the organization and resigned in the summer of 2021.

Only now, a few years removed from clinical medicine, can I begin to grasp how much the job shaped my worldview. I'm not in that battle anymore, but every so often, I catch up with a former colleague who is still on the front lines. After spending my twenties and thirties in the ER, my respect for career ER physicians and staff borders on awe. Not long ago, I met up with Parker, my former residency director. He has lived the emergency medicine life for over thirty years and is nearing retirement. We sipped a couple of beers and discussed the unique privileges and burdens of the job.

"They say there's no prayer more desperate and sincere than a prayer wailed in the ER," I recalled.

"There's no confession more honest or remorseful either," Parker added.

I nodded as I recalled the evening a man in his mid-fifties with chest pain and an abnormally fast heart rate arrived at the ER in an ambulance. With a look of doom on his face, he told me he had snorted cocaine and begged me not to let him die. Despite heroic efforts by our hospital's ER and cardiology teams, his final plea went unfulfilled. He died within half an hour of arriving at the hospital.

Some patients are already dead when they show up in the ER. Even more crushing are the deaths of patients who arrive clinging to life, the patients who even our best efforts cannot save. Witnessing these deaths is an inevitable aspect of every ER clinician's job, but that doesn't make it any easier. For me, the worst part of my job was having to tell someone that one of their very favorite people was dead. I think that every time I had to do it, my soul eroded a little.

Some of my toughest moments as a doctor will never leave my memory. An indelible example is the seven-year-old boy who died after being ejected from the back of a pickup truck in a highway accident. I'll never forget how the members of his family wailed, sobbed, shrieked, and fainted when I told them that the injuries the boy had sustained had killed him. The anguish felt so heavy and pervasive in that consultation room, I thought the paint on the walls might start weeping off and pooling on to the floor. But devastated people like those taught me a lot about what love really is. I began to understand that love means putting ourselves in positions that virtually guarantee pain in the future. I realize this is a morbid take, so now is probably a good time to mention that I believe moments of joy are what create love in the first place. I knew that each of those people to whom I broke terrible news had first experienced dozens, if not hundreds or thousands, of joyous moments; otherwise, they wouldn't have been crushed by my words.

Joy is the mother of love. Joy is addictive; biochemical and neurological pathways prove this. Moments of joy develop in us a strong desire to protect, preserve, and keep the source of our joy. If this take sounds a bit self-serving, that's because it probably is. We want "to have and to hold" the person who brings us joy forever. A unique beauty of this desire to preserve our source of joy is that it often compels us into incredibly selfless and altruistic action. I've refined my working definition of love over decades of serving many different roles on this Earth; each role has added something to how I think and what I believe. Now I'm a son, a brother, a scientist, a doctor, a husband, a father, and a teacher. With these roles as touchstones in my mind, I believe *love* is the *subconscious desire to preserve, protect, and keep a source of joy.*

Do I love my dog? Sure. She brings me joy and I want to preserve, protect, and keep her. Does she love me? Absolutely. She demonstrates her joy by exuberantly wagging her entire back half and giving me a hug and kiss every time I come home. It's been clear on many occasions that she wants to preserve and protect me too. A few years ago, we had to put down the first dog I ever owned. She was a sweet eleven-year-old lab who'd led a charmed life and brought our family unlimited joyful goofiness, but she was riddled with cancer in the end. I held that sweet girl and sobbed into her neck when she took her last breath; those of you who've been there know just how heartbreaking that moment is. It's almost impossible to believe that I've allowed myself to love another dog as much as my first one but, somehow, I have. An identical moment of pain lies down the road because I let myself love our new dog just as much. I'll break down, cry, and be generally emotionally wrecked for days, just like I was the first time. If the world weren't so full of examples, I would have a hard time imagining humans willfully signing on to receive the same crushing pain over and over again. Maybe it's an indication of just how addictive joy is or how desperately we seek connections with our fellow living things.

Romantic love, platonic love, and friendship are all branches of the same tree. I show my love for my wife, daughters, sisters, friends, students, and dog in very different ways because they all bring me joy in different ways. But in each instance, the root of the emotion is the same. They all bring me joy, so I want to preserve, protect, and keep them. Thinking of love this way explains why I wept watching my sixteen-year-old daughter drive her hand-me-down vehicle out of our driveway by herself for the first time. It had suddenly become much more difficult for me to protect, preserve, and keep her.

Yet now, the hope I feel has replaced the control I inevitably relinquished. I hope I have modeled good choices and responsible actions, and balanced them with ample amounts of spontaneity and freedom so that her life is even more joyous and meaningful than my own. I believe that my wife and I have loved both of our daughters with an abundance that justifies hope. So we will hope.

Chapter 4

ETERNAL LIFE

In the beginning God created the heavens and the earth.
—Genesis 1:1 (NIV)

How come in former lifetimes, everybody is someone famous?
—Crash Davis, *Bull Durham*

Buckle in—this chapter on eternal life isn't a short one. There probably aren't very many short chapters on eternal life; the idea itself seems like an oxymoron. I guess it makes the most sense to start at the beginning of my formal religious experience. My family baptized and raised me in the Catholic church, and I grew up immersed in its traditions and culture, accepting with certainty that the Holy Trinity was an all-knowing, all-powerful, three-faceted deity. Now that I'm growing old, I see a lifetime of experience in my rearview mirror. Even at this early stage of the book, it's probably clear to you that some sections are seasoned with unmistakably Christian herbs and spices. I've already employed a children's Bible school song and an Old Testament passage; that probably irked some readers. However, in this chapter, I'll break with Christian orthodoxy and submit that the Bible is essentially a book of myths. This suggestion is sure to upset a different cohort of readers.

It's taken a few decades, but I'm finally at peace with the fact that I can't be everyone's cup of tea.

On to the subjects of scripture and myth! Typically, myths are stories intentionally saturated with meaning and involving a combination of fictional characters and people who actually existed. Myths can also mix imagined events with events that undoubtedly occurred. Embellishing and decorating them to paint a moral picture or reveal a truth, we enhance each myth as we pass it down to the following generation. Myths can carry immense value; ironically, fictional works often illuminate deep truths of the universe.

Life of Pi is not only one of my favorite novels, but also a nearly perfect example of the creation, appeal, and value of myth. This work of fiction articulates two versions of one story. In the so-called "true" version, Pi loses his family in a shipwreck and drifts alone across the Pacific for months as he struggles for survival. In the narrator's far more beautiful, adapted version, a handful of zoo animals make it to Pi's life raft with him. Ultimately, after a series of violent exchanges, the only survivors are Pi and a Bengal tiger he must tame and keep at bay on a tiny raft for months. In the final pages of the book, we learn that the animals never existed at all and that the tiger is just an aspect of Pi's personality: Pi learned to become a tiger when his survival depended upon his own ferocity. "Which is the better story?" Pi asks at the conclusion of the book. I guess I've developed a *Life of Pi*[10] outlook on scripture and religion. The themes of many scriptural tales reveal inspiring and useful truths, but I believe their authors often added a couple tablespoons of creative license to enhance their effects and ensure that we would clearly interpret their meanings.

In the decades following the Council of Nicaea (325 CE), early Christian authorities chose the books of the modern Bible.[11] Nearly four hundred years after the death of Jesus, these early visionaries of the Christian faith reached a consensus on which writings would be included. The Bible remained relatively unchanged, albeit rare, for a few centuries after that. The arrival of the printing press in the fifteenth century enabled common people to read the Christian Bible, as well as propaganda that swept through Europe during the Protestant Reformation. The Protestants updated the original Christian (Catholic) Bible by removing a handful of Old Testament books, most notably the books of Maccabees.[12]

THIS CHANGE PRESENTS a significant problem for those Christians who view the Bible as the only definitive, trusted means of discovering truths about God. If the Bible's authors wrote under the divine influence of the Holy Spirit, and if early Christian authorities assembled those scriptures at the divine behest of the Holy Spirit, then why did Protestants later remove a handful of Old Testament books from the Bible? The fact that they removed these books means that Protestants must either believe that the Holy Spirit is fallible and capable of errors, or that early Christian leaders weren't acting exclusively under the divine, omnipotent influence of God while building the original Bible. If early Christian priests and clergy included some writings of the original Bible erroneously, then who is to say that other writings have not erroneously remained, while still other writings were erroneously omitted? I think it's misguided to deify the Bible itself; to me, it seems pretty hypocritical to worship a book whose sacred commandments instruct against idolatry.

The early Christian priest Arius of Alexandria maintained the belief that Christ was created instead of eternal; this meant that Christ could not be on equal footing with God himself. Arius was excommunicated and exiled by the Council of Nicaea; from then on, anyone espousing the Arian view was labeled a heretic.[13] I guess I am a heretic now. I doubt the divinity of Jesus. I doubt the Immaculate Conception. In my twenty years as a physician, I probably saw a hundred pregnant women who insisted there was no biological possibility that they were pregnant. Lo and behold, none of those conceptions wound up being immaculate ones. In every case, a human was the father. Two thousand years have passed since Christ's death, and we can't go back and test his DNA, or the DNA of his earthly father, Joseph. The definitive answer to the question of Christ's divinity is simply lost to history.

I imagine that the Council of Nicaea felt some pressure to ensure that Christianity would become a faith distinct from Judaism, instead of a sect of it. Establishing doctrinally that Jesus was eternal and on equal footing with God certainly accomplished that. I've read the Bible; some parts of it I've read dozens of times. At a point in my twenties, I was struck by how often in the Gospels Christ refers to himself as the "Son of Man" instead of the "Son of God." This realization gives me the same pause now as it did back then.

Even though he still respected and even adhered to many aspects of Christian doctrine, Abraham Lincoln doubted the divinity of Jesus.[14] The brilliant Dutch philosopher Benedictus de Spinoza famously described and defended the idea that God and Nature are one. God is Nature; Nature is God. This was a blasphemous stance for a seventeenth-century Jew to espouse and a brazen challenge to Jewish leaders of his time; to be sure, Spinoza's unconventional philosophy resulted in his expulsion from organized Judaism.[15] Alongside these philosophical role models, my mom's older brother, Tom, a retired Episcopal priest, has also strongly influenced my understanding of Christianity. The prayer he used to close his Sunday services has always resonated with me, even back when I had the hazy worldview of a teenager. "Be careful as you go out into God's creation, for it does not belong to you," Uncle Tom began. "Be gentle with yourself and others, for we are the dwelling place of the Most High. Be alert and be silent, for God is a whisper." Over the years, the idea that Nature and God are synonymous has grown on me. Maybe every member of humanity is a child of God. Maybe every human who ever lived was a child of God.

None of my intellectual challenges to Christian doctrine are to suggest that Christ was not a shining example for humanity; he certainly was. He spent his life fiercely advocating for the poor, castigating the greedy and pompous, challenging abusive power structures, and championing women's rights in ways that were far ahead of his time. I believe Jesus was a martyr who intended to inspire charity, kindness, and humility in his time and beyond. He rejected the established social and political order; powerful and wealthy people viewed him as a threat to both their cherished wealth and their formidable power.

My favorite Bible story is the one where Jesus flies into a rage, flipping over tables and chasing money-hungry merchants out of the temple. I think the central reason Christ was killed was that his charisma and revolutionary spirit made powerful people nervous. In time, revolutionary thinkers and activists such as Joan of Arc, Lincoln, Gandhi, Martin Luther King Jr., and Alexei Navalny would follow strikingly similar paths. Ironically, the same people who would have despised Christ in his own lifetime have commandeered a whitewashed version of his face and taken his quotes out of context; but they can't go back and change who he was when he walked the Earth. Dr. J.H. Holmes, a former Swarthmore College philosophy professor who interacted with Mahatma Gandhi on multiple occasions, summarized the spiritual and moral leader's views of contemporary Christianity in a quote first published in 1927: "I like your Christ, but not your Christianity."[16]

I do believe in eternal life, but probably not in the same sense as others believe in it. I don't think our semi-rotted corpses majestically rise out of the ground, sea, or ashes, then get patched up to resemble our younger selves. I don't believe that upon our deaths, our souls leave their earthen vessels to go sing and dance in the sky forever. Rather, I believe that other living organisms break down and use the organic materials of our bodies. The atoms and molecules we are made of get recycled. The credence these scientific principles add to Hindu and Buddhist teachings shouldn't be lost here. In a real sense, we are reincarnated; after we die, we come back as different living things. It's not a stretch to say that some of my carbon atoms previously belonged to Joan of Arc; at least a few of the trillions of amino acids found in my cells probably belonged to Thomas Paine a couple hundred years ago. The delightfully sneaky metaphysics tucked inside the *Bull Durham* quote at the beginning of this chapter also compel me to mention that many atoms in my body previously belonged to bacteria, earthworms, and dung beetles.

In 1789, Antoine Lavoisier brilliantly and meticulously proved that matter is neither created nor destroyed.[17] A precursor to every atom in our bodies was present at the beginning of the universe itself. About fourteen billion years ago, immediately preceding the Big Bang, all the matter in our current universe was condensed at a single point.[18] In a sense, we were all there the moment the universe pushed the Play button. To me, this realization validates the Buddhist principle of Universal Oneness. If we each began as one with everything, isn't the same true now? If God and Nature are one, as Spinoza suggests, then we were all there with God at the beginning. We were there when the universal laws of nature sprang into action; to pursue understanding of those universal laws, which we each unfailingly obey, is to seek God.

So if we don't go to an eternal jubilee in the sky after we die, is there an afterlife? I guess it depends on how we define the soul. I think most of us agree that the soul is not composed of matter—the soul is immaterial. To me, the soul and mind are synonymous occupants of the material brain; the immaterial soul exists inside the structural matter of the brain. Similarly, a family living inside a house is not part of the house but depends upon the structures and functions of the house to thrive. In this metaphor, the house is the brain, and the family is the soul. If disaster strikes and the house burns down, the family can escape. But now, to survive and thrive, the family will need a new house. I think the same goes for the soul. After inertia finally defeats the body, the soul can still survive as long as it finds a new house.

Christ's soul has eternal life. His words and actions have influenced the minds of billions of humans who have followed his teachings. Each person compelled to perform humble, charitable, selfless acts in his name helps carry his soul through the afterlife. Similarly, hundreds of millions of people have found motivation in the words and actions of Lincoln and King; both of their souls are poised to enjoy an eternal afterlife. For years,

I've also been inspired by the democratic ideals, writings, and actions of Thomas Paine. I'm certainly not alone. If I can influence the minds of family members and friends when I discuss the absurdity of hereditary monarchy and the evils of totalitarianism, then Thomas Paine's soul is carried through its afterlife.

Many individuals whose lives and teachings inspire us have long since lost their physical bodies to inertia. Yet by taking up residence in our brains, the souls of these leaders continue the fight for their respective causes. The soul achieves an afterlife when it enters a new brain and influences a new mind, inspiring a new living person to adopt an eternal cause. I'll discuss some of these eternal causes in more detail later. For now, it will suffice to mention that Lincoln's friend and colleague Edwin Stanton believed in them back when the fatally wounded hero drew his final breath. The moment that Lincoln was pronounced dead, Stanton remarked from his bedside, "Now he belongs to the ages."[19]

Chapter 5

FREE WILL

I don't know if we each have a destiny,
or if we're all just floating around accidental-like on a breeze.
But I think maybe it's both.
Maybe both is happening at the same time.
—Forrest Gump

If you can force your heart and nerve and sinew
To serve your turn long after they are gone,
And so hold on when there is nothing in you
Except the Will which says to them: "Hold on!"
—Rudyard Kipling, "If—"

Most people agree that both nature and nurture play significant roles in each human's identity, personality, and behavior. So where does free will fit in? I believe it's best to first explore nature and nurture before laying out my thoughts on free will and predestination. Let's begin with a few more nuts and bolts of biology. Each of our forty-to-fifty trillion human cells contains about six feet of DNA, tightly packed onto twenty-three pairs of chromosomes in the nucleus of the cell.[20] That DNA encodes every protein and enzyme that a human will use in their lifetime; about a hundred thousand separate genes are present in that DNA. As a result, much about each human's life is already decided before birth.

Cystic fibrosis (CF) is a genetic disorder caused by a gene mutation that encodes a faulty chloride channel in cell membranes. CF patients are plagued by gastrointestinal problems and dysfunction of the respiratory system. Although the average lifespan of a patient with CF has increased dramatically thanks to medical advances, it is still about twenty-five years fewer than that of someone without CF.[21] That's the result of nature, not human behavior. CF patients have the disease before they are even born, because it is encoded in their DNA. Sickle-cell disease is another example of a genetic disorder that, on average, shortens life expectancy by about twenty-five years. Its cause is a single DNA mutation that produces an abnormal protein in red blood cells. These abnormal red blood cells become misshapen and can pile up to block blood vessels, leading to intense, episodic pain and early organ failure.[22] Again, nature decides who will be affected before they are born.

All that said, understand that an individual patient's decisions directly impact the trajectory of their disease—this is true of any disease, genetic or not. Two otherwise healthy patients diagnosed with type 1 diabetes at the same age can have dramatically divergent courses. An insured patient with significant resources, ample understanding of their disease, advanced organizational skills, and the belief that they can take control of their illness will live a long, healthy life. On the other hand, an impoverished patient with inadequate support, low health literacy, and persistent feelings of powerlessness will suffer complications quite early. The second patient may develop failing vision and kidneys or need toe/foot amputations within the first few years of diagnosis. These hypothetical diabetic patients share the same physiology of disease—a pancreas that no longer makes insulin. The outcomes and quality of these patients' lives, however, couldn't be more different. Nature does not explain that difference—environment does. Before we can make empowered personal health decisions, we must first be aware of our own agency and then internally acknowledge our own worthiness.

While giving advice and options on smoking cessation might not be considered the role of an emergency physician, a specific patient encounter brought me the realization that reminding people of their own agency and willpower can have powerful effects. A longstanding smoker in his late twenties came in with wheezing, shortness of breath, and increasing cough. His chest X-ray was abnormal but didn't establish a definitive diagnosis of pneumonia or partial lung collapse. I sent him for a CT scan to help clarify things and nail down a treatment plan. It showed a developing pneumonia, but even more worrisome was the striking destruction of his lung tissue, consistent with emphysema. He didn't have the lungs of a twenty-eight-year-old; they were the lungs of a sixty-year-old, two-pack-per-day smoker. After I updated him on the radiologist's reading of his CT, I walked him over to the computer screen displaying the images of his lungs, scanning through them to offer explanation and context.

"Down here toward the bottom of your lungs, they look fairly healthy, like a twenty-eight-year-old set of lungs should look. But as we scroll up, you can see all of this black space inside the lungs. These are 'blebs,' and they don't do anything to help you get oxygen into your blood. This is lung tissue that's broken down by smoking—this destroyed lung tissue cannot do its job, and it's the reason that you get short of breath so often."

"Can we do anything to fix it?" he asked.

"Not really. The damage up here to this destroyed lung tissue has been done. The key is that we have to stop the damage from continuing. Your lungs need a ceasefire, or they will continue to deteriorate. You've got to stop smoking, or you won't be able to be active at all. You'll have to haul around an oxygen tank with you, not to mention that your risk of heart attacks and lung cancer will continue to climb."

He stood silently for a couple of seconds, looking gobsmacked. "I'm never smoking another cigarette. I'm throwing away the pack in my truck the minute I walk out of here, and I'm never buying them again."

I praised him for the decision, but knew that most smokers need a few tries before they quit successfully. So I bit my tongue and printed out his after-visit paperwork.

A couple of years later, he was back in the ER, not as a patient this time, but with an ill family member. He spotted me at my workstation and approached me, extending his hand to shake mine.

"Doc, I just wanted to thank you for planting the seed that got me to quit smoking. I haven't smoked a single cigarette since the last time I was here two years ago. You sent me the wake-up call I needed—those pictures made me realize I was killing myself with cigarettes."

That patient's story is one of millions offering a testament on the strength of will. In his case, will took on nature and nurture simultaneously, and defeated them both.

Since I just brought it up again, let's turn our attention to the subject of nurture. The environment where a human is raised is where nurture flexes its muscle. During the early waves of the COVID pandemic, my wife, a pediatrician, and I were both working on the front lines in clinical medicine. One evening after work, she told a story that struck me. Back then, everyone in medical facilities was masked at all times—everyone, that is, except the very young. Anyone who has ever tried to cajole a one-year-old into wearing a mask knows that the efforts are futile. Young children can't understand why something uncomfortable is necessary, and all the rules and reassurances in the world won't convince them to tolerate the nuisance. On that particular day, my wife, fully masked, walked into the clinic room of a three-month-old baby girl. As she always does upon greeting patients and families, my wife smiled as she made her entrance. Recall that the bottom half of her face was completely covered; her smile was hidden by the mask. Despite this, the baby smiled back at her. At three months of age, this tiny human recognized her doctor's smile when she could only see her eyes and forehead and immediately reciprocated the smile.

For the next few months, I made a point to see if I could repeat my wife's observation. I could. Every time I smiled at a baby who was old enough to exchange a social smile, but not yet old enough to have anxiety around strangers (this is a sweet spot of about three to eight months[23]), the baby returned the smile, *even though I was wearing a mask*! I was stunned by this illustration of just how social we humans are: A three-month-old human brain can recognize a smile even in the absence of its most defining feature—the shape of the mouth. Even more importantly, the young baby's brain receives the jolt of a dopamine, serotonin, and oxytocin cocktail when sharing a smile with someone else. Each time this happens, the budding neurologic pathway strengthens. With enough time and repetition, this subconscious response to a stimulus morphs into a lifelong social norm. The DNA blueprint for this pattern was always there, but it needed nurture to activate it. Throughout the course of a tragic, world-altering pandemic, rays of light like these occasionally shone through. Maybe stopping to wonder at human social predispositions and infant neurodevelopment allowed my wife and me to hear a faint whisper from God.

Recall from earlier that the mind and soul are synonymous. Within the physical matter of the brain, the mind (soul) engenders free will. The DNA of each cell encodes the blueprint to build the brain's structure, and beginning at birth, years of nurture construct an invisible but powerful mind inside that brain. By forming consciousness, the mind compels thoughts, beliefs, and actions. Yet since the mind is not composed of matter, no set of neuronal pathways or specific concentrations of neurotransmitters can unfailingly predict how a human will behave. The pendulum of free will versus predestination has swung back and forth between the two since the beginning of history. The answers lie somewhere in the middle; the true debate is about where, in between those two absolutes, we human beings spend our day-to-day lives.

Calvinist ideology heavily influences Christian beliefs and practices to this day.[24] Its early adherents believed that the soul of every human had its fate determined at, or even before, birth. Later Calvinist adaptations asserted that, due to the universality of sin, faith in Christ as God was the only path to preserve the soul.[25] For many past and present Christians, the strongest predictor of an individual's favor in the eyes of God is the earthly wealth, social class, and status of that particular person. Christianity surely doesn't own exclusive rights to this line of thinking. The caste system in India, which includes those of multiple faiths such as Hindus, Buddhists, and Muslims, is another illustrative example.[26] Yet one doesn't have to dig too deeply into Calvinist ideology to find the roots of "Manifest Destiny" and prosperity Christianity in the United States. By these doctrines, those who are stronger, wealthier, healthier, and better connected than others believe that they are favored by God. Even worse, the hungry, sick, and poor have often come to agree with the privileged few telling them that their suffering is because they are inferior in God's eyes.

Here, I want to shift gears slightly and examine the biology of skin color. Melanocytes are specialized skin cells that make a brownish pigment called melanin; every human has melanocytes. The melanocytes of lighter-skinned individuals produce a less darkly colored melanin. Darker-skinned individuals have melanocytes that produce a more darkly colored form of melanin. All of humanity exists on a spectrum ranging from those whose melanocytes produce only the light pigment (very pale-skinned individuals) to those whose melanocytes produce only the dark pigment (very dark-skinned individuals). An adult human has about three million melanocytes distributed across their skin surface; this means about 6 of every 100,000,000 human cells are melanocytes.[27] Melanocytes perform a very important function in absorbing ultraviolet (UV) radiation before it can damage cells located more deeply underneath, but they only make up a very tiny fraction of the entire human body. Examine the thickness of this page. That's how deeply melanocytes exist underneath the skin surface. As a physician with twenty years of clinical experience, I can assert with certainty that beneath that outer sheet of paper, every human looks the same. The tens of thousands of throats and ears I've examined, thousands of traumatic wounds I've managed, and hundreds of surgical cases and obstetric deliveries that I have performed, assisted in, and observed allow me to state it again as an absolute fact—we all look the same underneath the elastic sheet of paper covering our exteriors.

Despite the fact that pigment cells make up only 0.000006 percent of each of us, for centuries, societies have used their easily visible outward evidence to assign individuals their respective rights, worth, earning potential, and privileges. Hopefully, the math I've included here reveals the absurdity of this practice. When nature determines whether someone has a disease like cystic fibrosis or sickle-cell disease, that's biology. But when flawed people and societies misinterpret nature to justify their own abuses of others, that's a crime against humanity.

Over the course of history, the theory of total predestination has helped perpetuate hereditary monarchies and feudal systems; this theory has also enabled the wealthy and privileged to take advantage of the less fortunate while avoiding the long arm of the law. Colonial and early Americans used Calvinist tenets to rationalize their decisions to uproot and kill Native Americans; later, they used their catastrophic misinterpretations of the science of skin color to justify their decisions to enslave, abuse, and murder African people and their descendants. John Calvin may not have intended for his doctrine to become a weapon wielded by authoritarians, but it has served to maintain and increase their power at many times and places in human history.

When powerful abusers convince the abused to accept their station in life, to acquiesce, to no longer even hope for positive change, the abusers effectively seize control of the only force capable of removing them from power—the minds and souls of the oppressed. Now is a good time to pause and recognize that, for centuries and on many occasions, powerful people have warped the life, teachings, and story of Christ into formidable tools to suppress, intimidate, delegitimize, and even dehumanize the disadvantaged. That realization has humbled me; I believe it should humble every Christian who is willing and able to think critically.

As I move on to discuss free will, it's important to mention that there has been a recent push among some academics, intellectuals, and pseudointellectuals to "prove" that free will does not exist.[28] That is an opinion I resist with all my being. If free will doesn't exist, and therefore every event that occurs in the universe happens according to a predetermined script, then why does law exist? If free will doesn't exist, a murderer is going to murder—he has no choice—and no law or prospect of punishment can prevent him from killing. The concepts of right and wrong cannot exist in the absence of free will. How could anyone justify issuing a traffic ticket to someone who, since the moment of the Big Bang, has been destined to run a specific stoplight at a precise instant? Without free will, every criminal would be innocent by definition, and no punishment for any crime, however heinous, would be justified. When we stop believing in free will, we absolve every abuser in history of moral accountability. Whether they acknowledge it or not, those who assert that free will doesn't exist are making an argument to abolish the laws of society; the absence of free will would make law itself obsolete. Rendering laws, constitutions, and moral accountability obsolete is the coup de grâce of totalitarian regimes—doing so grants them absolute power to oppress, disenfranchise, kill, and steal without any concern for consequences.

If free will doesn't exist, then why have totalitarians throughout history worked so furiously to trample the will of the people? They do it because they know their efforts can suppress dissent; the pages of history books are filled with stories of autocratic dictators who, with varying degrees of success, were able to crush the collective will of their citizens. Pause and recognize that it is impossible to break something that does not exist. Authoritarians perceive that in the absence of free will there is no such thing as freedom. Once these authoritarians and their apologists convince the people that free will is an illusion, the step that follows is simple. If the people no longer believe in free will, they won't resist when their leaders nullify freedom of speech, freedom of the press, and freedom to protest.

Western democracies have built our rights and freedoms around the central pillar of free will. A diabolical totalitarian regime that has convinced a critical mass of people to no longer believe in free will is marching its entire population over the edge of a cliff and into an abyss. The fact that some of the marching citizens are wrapped in flags and singing patriotic songs while others are being marched at gunpoint is of no real consequence; the end result for all of them is the same. Beware anyone who peddles the "free will is an illusion" ideology—that person is merely a nihilistic tool of autocrats around the globe, whether he is getting paid by them or not. Free will is a defining feature of both human life and the human mind. Free will is a desire to resist inertia. To deny the existence of free will is to exalt the physical structure of the human brain while murdering the human mind and soul.

Free will survives because hope survives. Joan Walsh Anglund taught us: *"A bird doesn't sing because it has an answer. He sings because he has a song."*[29] The smiling three-month-old baby has no answers for the legion of problems, injustices, and abuses that plague the modern world. But the baby has a light. A three-month-old can deliver a powerful lesson on hope, as well as remind us of our own free will. If, at the right times, we can be alert and silent, we can hear the faint whispers of God.

Chapter 6

IDENTITY

Tomorrow people, where is your past?
–Ziggy Marley & The Melody Makers

Find out who you are
and do it on purpose.
–Dolly Parton

THIS CHAPTER WAS INITIALLY GOING to be about purpose, but purpose
has to wait for the next chapter. No one can grasp their purpose without
first establishing their own identity, so identity needs to come first here
as well. Both where and to whom we are born exert enormous cultural
influence on who we will become. Since our identities begin as shapeless
lumps of clay that are molded and revised over time, we should entirely
expect young people to experience years of internal strife, if not angst, as
they consider their purpose. One's identity must be sculpted fairly distinctly
before a clear purpose may be envisioned. In my ongoing interactions with
young people, I make a conscious effort to ask less about future career
plans and instead become more of a benevolent observer while students
discover themselves. When we ask adolescents what they'll be when they
grow up, they're bound to react with unspoken anxiety. When faced with
that unfair question, every kid should feel empowered to say, "I don't

know yet." I was in my forties before I figured out that I wanted to be a science teacher when I grew up.

Throughout my career in clinical medicine, I sought out opportunities to teach. Whether I was guiding terrified new interns at a patient's bedside or delivering lecture-style presentations to large audiences filled with experienced doctors, the teaching aspects of my clinical position never felt like work. In fact, opportunities to teach increasingly felt like reprieves from the crushing demands of clinical shifts in the ER.

About ten years into my career, I felt something had gone awry for me. I don't think I had quite reached burnout, but I was beginning to feel "off mission." I often caught my mind wandering to pursuits that might help me enjoy my job again. Considering the financial, temporal, and lifestyle commitments I'd made to become a residency-trained physician, the feeling of restlessness unnerved me. This conundrum is known as the "sunk cost" phenomenon. I'd spent eleven years past high school, borrowed tens of thousands of dollars, missed vacations and holidays, and lost touch with friends and family in the pursuit of a career I'd previously wanted; thinking of giving it away so soon seemed absurdly irresponsible. Any doctor who admits to having thoughts of straying away from clinical medicine is openly acknowledging an identity crisis. Since an identity crisis is typically considered a phase, and phases eventually pass, I think many professionals attempt to stay the course and outlast the phase. Years passed before I could even admit to my wife that I was experiencing an identity crisis; I had hoped it would resolve itself on its own. It never did.

Eventually, amid this crisis, I reached out to the high school biology and human anatomy teacher at the school my kids attended and asked if she could use any help in the lab on dissection days. Since my high school class in human anatomy and physiology was the first time I remembered feeling excited to learn, I figured maybe I should try to recreate that feeling, or at least help kindle that excitement in someone else. I kept my nerves in check while the anatomy teacher graciously welcomed and introduced me before the eleventh and twelfth graders who resumed their ongoing cat dissections. I hadn't been in an anatomy lab since medical school, but I felt renewed as I stood shoulder to shoulder with those students that day. This was an elective class; everyone was curious and relaxed. I circulated from table to table, asking focused questions to help the students identify anatomical structures.

"What is this thing right here?" a goggled and ponytailed girl asked while pointing her probe at the ureter.

"Where does it come from?" I offered.

She traced the structure upward. "The left kidney," she replied.

"And where does it go?" She slid the probe downward until it encountered a spherical structure in the pelvis.

"It goes to the blad—it's the ureter!" We exchanged a gloved fist bump, and I moved on.

A tall, lanky kid coaxed me over from a nearby table. He was examining the aortic arch and the structures branching from it. I got a little nervous because there were only two branches arising from his cat's aortic arch, and humans have three. After suffering a few seconds of impostor syndrome, I recognized the difference and was able to determine the anatomy.

"I see the brachiocephalic and left subclavian. But what's this one?" he questioned with his probe pointing to the left common carotid artery.

"Where does it come from?" I asked again.

"It branches off the brachiocephalic, which comes off the aortic arch," he quickly responded.

"And where does it go?" I volleyed back, sticking with the same effective script.

"It travels up the left side of the neck and to the head," he replied while tracing the artery upward. "It's the left carotid artery!"

"That's right—the left common carotid artery," I agreed while exchanging another fist bump.

Where does it come from? Where does it go? Those are two incredibly useful questions when identifying anatomical structures. With a little introspection, the same questions can help us understand our own identities so that we may purposefully plot our individual paths. Where do I come from? Where am I going?

Identity typically operates in the subconscious; it's there influencing our thoughts and decisions, but we aren't aware of *how* it influences those thoughts and decisions. In times of crisis and soul-searching, however, we can pull identity into the frontal lobe and actively examine who we are. I've made both terrific and questionable decisions in my life, but I've never once regretted a choice I made after first stopping to examine my own identity. I still remember the patient encounter that compelled me to consider leaving the ER and taking a job in urgent care. I was in the ER working with a twenty-something man who had cut his hand pretty badly with a utility knife. After obtaining all the standard information, such as when he'd gotten his last tetanus booster shot, which hand was his dominant one, and how long ago his injury had occurred, I sat down to inject the anesthetic (numbing medicine) and wash out his wound so that I could repair it with sutures. He had a pretty intense needle phobia, and he asked if I could give him a Valium before injecting the anesthetic. I reassured him that I would be as gentle as possible, and once the anesthetic was in, he wouldn't feel a thing. He tolerated the injection very well, admitting, "You were right, Doc. That wasn't bad at all."

As I was irrigating the wound with water, we both saw a pair of feet appear just below the curtain of his exam room. He recognized the feet as his wife's. "Let's freak her out," he whispered with a smile. "She knows I can't stand needles, so I'm gonna start screaming and begging you to stop."

I grinned back. "I'm game, as long as you think she won't get *too* upset."

He started shouting and writhing on the stretcher. "Stop! Stop, please! It hurts too bad. I'm gonna pass out!"

"Hold still!" I yelled back. "Don't be a baby—it's almost over!"

His wife threw the curtain open and stomped in with an incredulous look on her face. "What are you doing to him? What is wrong with you?" The patient smiled and started chuckling, and his wife's shoulders relaxed before she grinned sheepishly and slid into a chair. The three of us shared a rowdy laugh before I got to work placing the sutures and bandaging up the patient's hand.

I returned to my computer to write the encounter note and print his discharge papers. I was happy to have received a reprieve from the crush of work stress by connecting with a fun-loving patient. A thought hit me: "You know—you don't have to work in an ER to be a doctor." I suddenly realized that I could enjoy interacting with fun-loving patients like him in several different, lower-pressure clinical settings, not only in the ER. He was the patient who empowered me to change my professional environment from ERs to urgent care clinics; he helped me recognize and nail down a key component of my identity. He illuminated the fact that, for me to feel satisfaction at work, I need to connect with people, often through shared frivolity and laughter.

With each passing day, month, or year of life, our identities evolve. Each trip we make around the sun adds another chapter to where we came from and establishes the trajectory we follow. When I arrived at Virginia Tech, I was an eighteen-year-old hillbilly with a chip on his shoulder who was pretty good at math. I was also a child of divorced parents and a lackluster athlete. At forty-eight, I'm still all of those things, but I'm also a doctor with twenty years of clinical experience behind him. I'm a husband and a dad; I'm a coach and a science teacher. I haven't lost the facets of my identity I owned when I was a college freshman; I've just added to them.

Dozens of variables had to align for me to get into medical school, but I was the central figure manipulating those variables. Once I had gotten in, I had to put in the effort to become a doctor before it could become an aspect of my identity. It's tough to describe the self-discipline and sacrifice of a medical student and resident. Thousands of hours spent studying and training bring the highly intentional consequence of creating selfless servants; our identities are powerfully shaped over the course of those years. Similarly, before I could take on the identity of a teacher, I had to first choose to leave my established profession and commit myself to teaching young people instead.

For many who are considering a career change, the "sunk costs" mentioned earlier prove to be insurmountable forces of inertia. Thankfully, I was able to overcome these forces, but my decision to do so was not without uncertainty and angst. Somehow, at a critical crossroads in my life, I mustered up enough hope and courage to choose a path that led to a more satisfying personal and professional life. But a handful of crucial moments aren't all that shape the lives we create; dozens of times per day, we each have the chance to decide where we are going and who we are going to be. These choices are both influenced by and formative forces of identity.

My dad is nearing eighty. He is a true creature of habit. I remember him taking us to a church pancake breakfast one Sunday between the 8 a.m. and 11 a.m. masses. We could choose from chocolate chip, banana, and blueberry pancakes; there were strawberries and whipped cream to put on the pancakes. No one was shocked when dad ordered the plain pancakes with butter and maple syrup.

He grew up poor and maintained the frugality of his parents; he had a tough time even imagining such wild pancake variations. This background should help explain why Dad didn't have the luxury of getting into a swimming pool very often in his youth. I'm not sure how old he was when he learned to swim. When we were kids, my sisters and I quickly realized that he barely could. In those days, his most effective stroke was this slapstick, no-arms form of backstroke that he employed to inch forward while his knees furiously pumped in and out of the water, as if he were riding a bike as fast as he could. My sisters and I found it hilarious and loved to smoke him in the pool at the end-of-season swim team party where the kids got to race the adults. Now, he goes to the pool three or four times per week and, for an old guy, has become the picture of graceful swimming. Swimming has enabled him to keep up the healthy exercise habit he developed in his thirties while also preserving his joints. He has found something he loves and will talk to you about swimming for as long as you can stand it.

"I figure I'm the top male seventy-five-plus swimmer in town," he bragged a while back when we were chatting on the phone.

"You probably are. I'd put my money on you," I replied, not blowing smoke in the least.

In his late seventies, my dad wanted to become a champion swimmer. In creating a new routine, he became one. My dad is an example that, regardless of age or habits, we each can choose to change how we think of ourselves. Even though my dad probably couldn't have imagined it in his youth, he now sees himself as a swimmer. Identity is never completely fixed, not even for a creature of habit like my dad.

Chapter 7
PURPOSE

*People say that what we're all seeking is a meaning for life. I don't
think that's what we're really seeking. I think that what we're seeking is
an experience of being alive, so that our life experiences on the purely
physical plane will have resonances within our own innermost being
and reality, so that we actually feel the rapture of being alive.*
—Joseph Campbell, *The Power of Myth*

*No one is useless in this world ... who lightens the burden
of it for any one else.*
—Charles Dickens, *Our Mutual Friend*

CALLING THIS CHAPTER "THE MEANING OF LIFE" felt a little preten-
tious, especially when I don't feel terribly close to having it figured out.
Since each individual exists in their own reality, the meaning of life varies
greatly; it's tough to assert that any one belief carries more weight than
another. I don't think the universe needs a purpose to exist, but it's an
unassailable fact that the most memorable and transformative humans
in history led their lives with a sense of purpose.

Fortunately for me, I don't need to spend my waking hours concerned
with whether my family can access healthcare or where we will find our
next meal. I've never had to spend a single night in a home without indoor

plumbing. If you haven't appreciated it already, I strongly suggest spending a few minutes examining Mazlow's hierarchy of needs pyramid. Most of us, including me, spend our days near the top of the pyramid; we seek connections, the respect of others, and creative accomplishments.[30] We have the time and energy to pursue the meaning of life. But unless we spend some time with others who struggle to meet more basic needs for housing, nutrition, and healthcare, it is impossible for us to appreciate their day-to-day challenges. After nearly five decades on Earth, I believe there are only two truly noble human pursuits: to honestly seek truth with no aim other than finding it, and to improve the life of someone less fortunate.

When Euclid enumerated the foundations of plane geometry, he was describing truths from the natural world.[31] To seek a truth about the natural world and universe is to seek God; to discover a natural truth is to discover an aspect of God. Where God and Nature are one, the artificial dichotomy between religion and science becomes a merely political one; it has no defensible basis in the seminary or the laboratory. The truths of Nature aren't discovered in silos; discoveries that change the world are frequently the result of multiple relentlessly curious minds working independently, never meeting in the same laboratory. Einstein's discovery of relativity was actually a cross-generational collaboration of truth seekers including Lavoisier, Michael Faraday, and Lise Meitner;[32] the accomplishment fittingly transcended time and space. I don't believe God seals the truths of the universe away in a vault to forever protect them from prying human eyes. I think those truths are meant for us to discover. Having the capability and resources to pursue the truths of the universe is possibly the greatest privilege a human can possess.

Carl W. Buehner once told us, "They may forget what you said, but they will never forget how you made them feel."[33] A solid biological foundation supports this statement; the deeper, more primitive areas of the human brain are essential in synthesizing human emotions like fear and love. As a result, the moments that trigger these powerful emotions are difficult to erase. Contrast these foundational areas of the brain with the region tasked with remembering the exact words and syntax of a sentence you heard spoken to you years ago. Unless that sentence generated a significant emotional response, it's unlikely that you remember it with unfailing clarity.

When I was younger, Buehner's quote stressed me out a bit because I thought it had to do with the importance of making a good first impression. Insecure twenty-three-year-old me took his words to mean that if I rubbed someone the wrong way, they would hate me forever. I'm a little more emotionally mature now, and the nuance of the quote hits differently. Now I see it as a reminder that I can pretty much always help someone less fortunate than I am to feel better. I can help an anxious student understand a new concept by taking the time to help them navigate their individual obstacles to comprehension; I can make sure a lonely person feels seen as long I'm observant enough to recognize loneliness; I can help a hungry person feel full by pausing to share my abundance; and I can help a hopeless person feel loved when I switch out of a mode of selfish, task-oriented achievement. Each of the generous acts listed above share a couple of common threads: recognizing humanity everywhere it exists and consciously connecting with that humanity in others. My undergraduate university, Virginia Tech, has the most shamelessly simple and humanistic motto I've come across: *Ut Prosim*. Latin for "that I may serve," the motto is a humble reminder that we can only find our purpose through serving humanity.

I was ten or eleven and visiting Washington, DC, the first time I saw a real homeless person. This isn't because I grew up wealthy. In the 1980s, you just didn't come across any homeless people in the hills, coalfields, and rail yards of Southwest Virginia. An economic backbone was in place to support the growth and sustenance of an impressive array of towns, schools, and businesses. Not once in my hometown did I see someone begging on a street corner or huddled under a highway overpass. Volumes have been written on the disappearance of the middle class in America, and I'm not going to dissect this shift here; I just want to offer some context on why it felt so striking and disorienting for me to see that emaciated and barefoot Black man with tufts of white hair on each side of his head.

I can still picture him. He was wearing a ragged, used-to-be-white shirt and beat-up navy-blue pants. He held a sign with "Help" scrawled on it, and sat on a square of cardboard right next to the main thoroughfare of the sidewalk. Shock froze my gaze upon him as my mom led my sister and me along to our first destination of the morning. After we had passed a few yards in front of him, I watched someone hand him a sandwich or biscuit wrapped in foil. I remember feeling a small measure of comfort that at least he wasn't going to starve that day. Absorbing the history and grandeur of the monuments was impossible after that; I was too rattled. Later that evening when we were settling into bed, my disbelief morphed into devastation, and I broke down. My mom tried her best to gently but truthfully answer all my questions about how God and the world could let things like that happen.

My daughters grew up in the city; as soon as they were able to hold their heads up, they started seeing homeless people on the street corners through their passenger windows. A few years ago, it struck me how few questions they asked about homeless people and homelessness. I think they accepted these realities at a far younger age than I did. Another troubling moment followed this realization—that they would grow up without the idealism that I had developed as a child. I started to wonder just how much empathy and human compassion have faded over the last few generations. Has the ubiquitous presence of poverty granted it mass societal acceptance? Is it too late for us to save the human compassion that helps to define us as a species?

Although I'm no longer a practicing Catholic, the Prayer of Saint Francis is still my favorite religious prayer. "Make me an instrument of your peace," the prayer begins. Francis of Assisi was a prominent thirteenth-century Catholic leader who gave up all his material belongings and humbly devoted his life to serving the poor. Most modern sources agree that the prayer was unlikely to have been written by Saint Francis himself, but rather in homage to him.[34] Many years after Saint Francis's death, someone was inspired to create a message to extend Saint Francis's legacy. The prayer they wrote is helping to carry his soul through its afterlife by calling subsequent generations to service.

In an earlier chapter, I brought up the idea of eternal causes. An eternal cause is one that we can never fully achieve; to adopt an eternal cause is to enlist in a battle that will not be won in our lifetime. This seems discouraging at first blush and, throughout modern history, miserable cynics and nihilists around the world have capitalized on this seemingly depressing realization. We've all heard nihilistic comments like this:

- "We will never end poverty worldwide; you're wasting your time trying to fight it."
- "The world is never going to be fair. It's senseless to work for equality."
- "Just let Russia do whatever the hell they want."

The answers to these riddles are surprisingly simple. When someone adopts an eternal cause and an infinite mindset, they aren't fighting to defeat poverty—they are using their time, energy, and resources to help lift *individual people* out of poverty. Helping just a single impoverished person advances that eternal cause. Empowering just one disadvantaged individual to achieve upward social mobility advances the eternal cause of equality. Working to sustain a free and independent Ukraine advances the eternal cause of democracy. Over the years, I've learned that nihilistic arguments are highly intentional traps people set to distract servants and activists from advancing their eternal causes. Debating a nihilist is akin to giving medicine to a dead person; it's a waste of time, energy, and resources.

My career in emergency medicine granted me a position to simultaneously seek truth and improve the lives of the less fortunate. Dozens of times per day, a suffering person showed up seeking clarity and relief; pretty much everyone who arrives at the ER is having one of the worst days of their lives. Using scientific principles and training to tease signal away from noise and discover truth amid chaos felt immensely gratifying. Providing just a few minutes or hours of relief to a patient desperately seeking it helped me put compassion into action, even if it was impossible for me to heal everyone.

Teaching science to young people is rewarding and validating in different ways. If just a dozen of the hundred or so students I lead each year employ a concept I introduced to build a greater understanding of universal truths, and just half of those then go on to use that understanding to improve the lives of others, then my impact multiplies. In middle school, the situation on the ground is both literally and figuratively messy. Pencils are scattered on the floor and there are wadded-up tissues on the tables; a kid is having meltdown over their test performance; a group of friends is at odds with one another; chairs aren't pushed in; the whiteboards have been hijacked by teenage vandals with markers; forgotten sweatshirts and water bottles litter the tables and floor. But every so often I pause, pull back, and examine the big picture of what is really happening there. The aerial view never fails to humble and renew me. The kids are discovering their talents and learning how to apply concepts across academic disciplines; they're figuring out how to advocate for themselves and how to be good friends. They're feeling the satisfaction that comes with helping someone else. They're becoming their adult selves, and I get to join my new teacher friends and be there for it. What a humbling privilege it all is.

Chapter 8

WORK

What we really want to do is what we are really meant to do.
When we do what we are meant to do,
money comes to us, doors open for us,
we feel useful, and the work we do feels like play to us.
—Julia Cameron, *The Artist's Way*

When work is a pleasure, life is a joy.
—Maxim Gorky, *The Lower Depths*

For physicists, work means "a force acting upon an object that causes displacement of that object."[35] While there aren't many nonphysicists who would define work this way, I think it's helpful to understand that work, by definition, *moves something*. It's easy to see that those who use their muscles in their day-to-day vocations are engaging in work; they are moving things for dozens of hours per week. But a more abstract interpretation of work also applies; it might mean turning an idea into action, changing the direction of a project, or applying resistance to slow a venture down and correct its course around impending pitfalls. By this rationale, work, like life, clearly opposes inertia. It may seem strange that, a few sentences into a discussion of work, I haven't mentioned money, salary, or other remuneration. To truly work is to use one's energy to oppose inertia and move things.

I was probably in my late twenties or early thirties when I realized that my view of money is different from that of most other people. The experiences of my adolescence are the likely roots of my uncommon conception of money; since they are the primary determinants of how I value a job, I think it's important for me to discuss these experiences now. I don't ever remember drawing any deep satisfaction from the number on a paycheck or W-2 form. In some ways, I'm sure this relatively neutral response reflects the luxury of never experiencing poverty or consistently missing meals. Again, this is not to insinuate that I grew up wealthy. Until my parents split up when I was twelve, they collaborated to secure a middle-class upbringing for my sisters and me. My dad worked as a traveling sales rep for a paper company; he called on every grocery store in Southern West Virginia, Southwest Virginia, Northeast Tennessee, and Eastern Kentucky. My mom was an elementary school teacher who later became a principal; at home, I got my ass whipped with a paddle of the exact specifications as the ones that were used in her school. Growing up, my sisters and I were clothed and well fed, and each of us was able to participate in a few after-school sports.

Every summer, our family rented a room somewhere close to the ocean in Myrtle Beach on the coast of South Carolina. If you've never been, Myrtle Beach is a commercialized strip of coastline that has attracted the families of Appalachian and Rust Belt wage earners for the past two or three generations. While the golfing there has earned a world-class reputation over the years, Myrtle Beach still isn't a destination for socialites or the ultrarich; it's a colorful, congested, and often-tacky party spot for teenagers and families wanting to play Putt-Putt, gorge on seafood buffets, and drive go-karts. Growing up, my sisters and I bodysurfed, built sandcastles, and watched the prop planes pull banner signs across the sky for an entire week each summer. On most of our vacation weeks, we met new friends from towns in Ohio or Pennsylvania that were similar to ours and became pen pals with a few of those kids. Each morning, we fought over who got the Apple Jacks and Cocoa Krispies from our Kellogg's multipack of cereal, but our parents took us out to eat every night. While we never saw the inside of a posh hotel, we didn't know enough to care about what we might have been missing.

On one of those beach trips, at about age nine or ten, I had my first beer. Late in the afternoon, I walked up from the ocean and picked up what I thought was a coke. Unfortunately for me, my mom had been smoking, and the can was filled with more ashes than soda; I coughed, choked, and gagged on the acrid sludge. Desperate to provide me with some mercy, mom reached in the cooler to find that the only drink left was an ice-cold Old Milwaukee. She opened it and handed it to me; I took a few gulps to recover. I've had more than a few refreshingly timely beers in my life, but I don't think any of them tasted better than the domestic swill that washed down those cigarette ashes.

Landlocked in Appalachia for most of the year, our annual trip to Myrtle Beach represented one of the two occasions per year that our family got to enjoy shrimp; Christmas Eve was the other. My dad's extended Italian family would get together at cousin Ernie's house for a huge dinner in between the afternoon and midnight masses at Sacred Heart Catholic Church. A couple of relatives lived in St. Augustine, and they always hauled up a cooler full of shrimp with them to complete the holiday feast. There were shrimp-cocktail appetizers and shrimp boiled in the thin red sauce that Ernie's mom Bonnie poured over angel-hair pasta. Christmas Eve was, without fail, the best meal of the year, and a highlight of my childhood. Shrimp and fresh seafood were such rare delicacies back then that even today, I feel that sense of celebration every time they make an appearance on my table.

Looking back, my parents lived a typical "American dream" that millions of their fellow baby boomers enjoyed in the 1970s and '80s. My dad grilled cheap cuts of steak on summer Saturday nights. I remember going to the matinee to watch all three Indiana Jones movies shortly after each was released. Our whole family attended high school football games together, especially over the years when my sister was on the sidelines cheering. Occasionally, my dad came across tickets to a Virginia Tech game; I would tag along with him on the hour-and-a-half trip east to Blacksburg and watch the scrappy but marginally talented Hokies of the 1980s. If the American dream represents the realization of upward social mobility, then in those days, both of my parents were "living the dream." By objective measures, they both enjoyed better lives than they had experienced growing up. My mom was raised on a farm with five siblings; my dad is the son of a schoolteacher and a grocer who worked like hell to pull their family out of poverty that began in a shanty perched upon a hillside next to a set of railroad tracks.

Very few things last forever; maybe nothing at all does. Eventually, our family's American dream fell apart; our parents split up when my twin sister and I were eleven or twelve. My older sister had just graduated from high school and been accepted to the University of Virginia. That summer, my parents began having increasingly frequent conversations on the front porch; this was a strange new pattern. My twin sister and I were curious, so we started eavesdropping on them. It didn't take long for us to understand that the topics they were discussing were the mechanics and details of their impending divorce. We wrote and signed a joint letter to my mom and dad, begging them not to separate. They probably cried when they read it, but it didn't accomplish our goal of preventing their split. A couple of weeks later, I went to Myrtle Beach again with my mom and sisters, but my dad stayed behind. When we got back, some of our furniture was gone, and he had moved out to an apartment a couple of miles away.

The sudden change was initially tempered by geographic proximity; my twin sister and I lived with our mom most of the time, but we were able to stay with our dad often. A year or so passed with the two of us splitting time between our parents. Then my mom got remarried and planned to move to the suburbs of Orlando. Somewhat begrudgingly, my sister and I left with her and started eighth grade at a middle school about five hundred miles away from where we'd lived our first thirteen years. Central Florida wasn't all bad—it's home to the happiest place on Earth, after all. Our stepdad lived far more comfortably than we were used to; there was a pool in the backyard of our new house. We went out to eat a lot more often than before, and he and my mom owned Orlando Magic season tickets. Our stepdad was a jovial, charismatic guy who shared generously with my sister and me and helped us with our math homework.

Although we had been transported into a life of greater privilege, my sister and I weren't happy. We missed the connections we had forged over the years back home; making new friends as a young teen is difficult and stressful. I think there's a shred or two of poetry in the fact that now, more than thirty years later, I teach kids who are the same age that I was when I experienced one of the most tumultuous years of my life. So it's easy to see why I have a soft spot for the kids who transfer into our school at the start of their eighth-grade year. After a few months in Florida, my sister and I made the decision to move back to Virginia and live with my dad. My mom was crushed; I don't remember ever seeing her cry the way she did when she dropped us off back home and told us goodbye.

The life my sister and I moved back to was far less abundant than what we'd left in Florida; to be sure, things were noticeably leaner than when we had lived in Virginia before our parents split. Our dad was on the road a lot. By the time we were in high school, my sister and I had learned how to do our own laundry, a skill that made our future transitions to college life far easier. Dad did his best to keep the refrigerator and pantry cabinets pretty well stocked, but pickings were slim at times. He made an incredible homemade marinara sauce (still does), and there was often a lasagna baking in the oven or leftover in the fridge; his homemade mac and cheese was a crowd-pleaser every time. Still, some nights the fridge seemed to be filled with more condiments than food; dinner on those nights was typically a fried bologna sandwich with mustard or some instant ramen. My dad's younger sister invited us over every Sunday for a home-cooked

Italian feast; she made delicious homemade meatballs, Italian sausage, manicotti, and a marinara sauce with pork ribs as the base. On more special occasions, she would spend the afternoon making handcrafted gnocchi from scratch and then serve them up for supper. Although my aunt never mentioned it, she must have known that her brother never signed up to raise two hungry teenagers by himself. So no matter what happened during the week, my sister and I could always count on a home-cooked feast at our Aunt Marcia's house on Sunday.

When my sister and I decided to leave Florida and come live with our dad, I don't think either of us took money or creature comforts into account. Except for our mom, all of our relationships were back in the hills of Virginia; there weren't enough dinners out, trips to theme parks, or NBA games in Orlando to even approach the power of those connections. I think the changes I experienced in my early teen years solidified my belief that non-tangible things are far stronger and much more important than money.

An overused adage tells us that money can't buy happiness. While I agree to a certain extent, I think the adage needs some editing; no one who uses that phrase is actually living in poverty. Money may not guarantee complete happiness, but it's virtually impossible to be happy without enough money to prevent hunger, homelessness, and despair. I've lived through phases of life that 95 percent of the world's population would consider opulently abundant, and I've "endured" other stretches that millions of Americans would consider unbearably lean. But through all these stages, I always had at least enough resources to survive and thrive. I've never had to work a job for the sole purpose of staving off poverty; I had enough opportunities for me to try out jobs and choose one I thought I might like. The gift of this reality has enabled me to view work not as my only weapon to beat back starvation and homelessness, but rather as a source of meaning, fulfillment, and joy.

Like many teens in the 1990s, I mowed yards for cash. My first paycheck-earning job was at my hometown Kroger, where I bagged groceries and pushed buggies inside from the parking lot. In the ensuing years, I worked as a lifeguard, managed a pool for a summer, worked as an orderly at our local hospital, and waited tables. This collection of jobs taught me how to accept direction, feedback, and criticism, as well as how to effectively handle people who were upset. Being an ER doctor depends on thousands of hours of education and training, but I'm not kidding when I say that learning the strategy and process of waiting tables in a restaurant was equally useful. Meeting the rapidly shifting needs of individuals at different stages in their lives while simultaneously shepherding the whole flock is the essence of emergency medicine; effective restaurant servers can masterfully combine these tasks.

People say that work shouldn't define a person, but I don't mind at all if someone defines me through the lens of my work. An individual's approach to work is a telling reflection of their personality, outlook, and even philosophy. Over time, those different jobs constantly stoked my curiosity and helped me establish a love of learning; each job enabled me to use my energy to create movement and progress. Being an ER doctor taught me that, sometimes, even herculean efforts can't change the course of an injury or disease. The story of the young chain-smoker who committed to quit cold turkey is the flip side of that same lesson; words and actions that are seemingly insignificant at the time are often enough to change a life for the better. Teaching young people has reminded me that I have the power to establish a culture of emotional safety; when I do, the kids respond with impressive effort and boundless creativity.

Chapter 9

STRENGTH

Nothing is so strong as gentleness,
nothing so gentle as real strength.
—Saint Francis de Sales

Power tends to corrupt
and absolute power corrupts absolutely.
—Lord John Dalberg-Acton, letter to Mandell Creighton (1887)

I THOUGHT OF A FEW POTENTIAL titles for this chapter. "Resilience" would have worked; either "determination" or "resolve" would have fit as well. Calling this chapter "grit," "honor," or "integrity" would have allowed me to follow with paragraphs virtually identical to the ones below. However, I settled on "strength" because its scientific definition holds up well across the many contexts in which we use the word. In physics, mechanical strength is "a material's ability to withstand various external forces without breaking or yielding."[36] The composition of a metal alloy or plastic largely determines its strength. For me, it's right on the nose to apply the same definition and concept to humans. An individual's strength grows internally; it depends on the identity they embrace and the beliefs they hold tightly. I'm not suggesting that someone who possesses impressive strength can withstand any and every situation or stressor; circumstances and difficulties can arise that would inevitably break or kill each of us. I'm merely submitting that humans develop variable capacities to tolerate and even defy turmoil, uncertainty, and hardship.

When I think of strength, US Navy SEALs, Marine Corps Special Forces, and Army Green Berets immediately come to mind. I don't have the composition to complete that training, but many others have shown it. While I like to think I'm pretty strong, I'm not elite-warrior strong. I never was. Similarly, when Alexei Navalny voluntarily returned to Russia after surviving the poisoning that nearly killed him, it became clear that he was made of tougher stuff than most of us. He undoubtedly knew that he'd undergo a sham trial and spend the rest of his foreshortened life in prison, but he went back home anyway. Navalny's eternal cause was to inspire his fellow Russians to resist totalitarianism and settle for nothing less than liberty and democracy; he didn't believe he could fulfill his own purpose without voluntarily returning to face his enemy. Because his example of strength lives on, so does his eternal cause.

Though they may seem synonymous, power is a very different human attribute than strength; power does not arise directly from a person's internal composition, or from the inner fortitude they develop through practice over time. Power is much more situational than strength—a Fortune 500 CEO may wield fearsome power in the boardroom, only to be repeatedly derided and mocked by their teenage daughter at home. Physics defines power as force multiplied by distance over time. An object is powerful when it can impart great force across a great distance in a short amount of time. Let's apply a new example here to help direct our analysis from physics to civics and geopolitics: the United States Constitution assigns an incredible amount of power to the commander in chief of the armed forces. Within mere minutes, a president can mobilize thousands of military personnel stationed on different continents. That's power—moving a massive force across a long distance in the time it takes to make a phone call.

Recognize that this power exists regardless of the president's strength of character. In a perfect world, those with substantial power would first develop strength by shaping their beliefs, values, and identity through decades of lived experiences and conscious thought. A leader with inner strength humbly accepts power as an honorable burden. But everyone knows the world is far from perfect; the most dangerous leaders in human history have been those with immense power and weak character. All too often, terrified narcissistic nihilists remind us how they behave when they hold power. Those who relentlessly pursue power for no purpose other than to achieve and increase it never develop strength; they become hollowed-out, paranoid caricatures who lead their organizations and societies to ruin.

Honor and strength of character are so tightly interwoven that I don't think we can possibly tease them apart. If honor, or integrity, means doing the right thing even when no one is looking, then those who act honorably reinforce the assertion that strength comes from within. Since the ease of access to information, artificial intelligence, and famous examples of moral bankruptcy have opened gray areas in the realm of acceptable academic conduct, our school's honor code has taken on a livelier and more central role in daily assignments and discussions. I think our school's entire faculty understands that fostering the development of each student's character is far more vital than any lab activity or lesson we can conduct.

Recently, I handed my students back a graded test on the respiratory and circulatory systems that almost all of them had found pretty challenging; the average score was significantly lower than it was for previous tests and quizzes. We reviewed the test as a class to help the students correct what they'd missed. A couple of the kids caught grading errors I'd made and brought them to my attention; I praised them for their self-advocacy and promised to add those points into the gradebook. A bright, quiet, bespectacled girl called me over to mention that her score was too high— she had missed a question that wasn't tallied into the total.

"I was wrong here. I put that *red blood cells* deliver oxygen to the heart muscle instead of the *coronary arteries*, and you didn't count off for it," she confessed.

Humbled, I praised her for her honesty. "I decided that 'red blood cells' is also a correct answer. They do carry oxygen to the heart muscle, after all."

Being a teacher often brings glimmers of hope like these, as long as I remain alert for them. Younger generations haven't universally accepted the "might makes right" and "it's only cheating if you get caught" attitudes and worldviews that surround them. Honesty and integrity can survive among people who are brave enough to believe in themselves and resist inertia.

I challenge the assertion that nihilists believe in nothing. There are two concepts in which nihilists have immense faith: power and inertia. Since inertia leads to death, nihilists certainly believe in death as well. Newtonian laws demonstrate that bodies exerting immense gravitational force attract less-massive bodies toward them. Cosmic black holes serve as an illustrative metaphor for totalitarian regimes. Their incredible mass exerts such gravitational force that not even light can escape.[37] Totalitarian states function like geopolitical black holes; the nihilistic ruling regime achieves such a degree of power that not even the light of truth is able to escape its force. Corrupt acts and unwritten abusive policies perpetuate themselves under a shroud of darkness; each time a criminal goes unpunished, he is further enabled and empowered. Power seizes wealth, and more wealth further increases the force that the ruling regime exerts over the people. This is the exact recipe employed during the Putinist takeover in Russia; it has more than its share of American adherents, as well as a notable South African one. Once they've amassed enough wealth, totalitarian nihilists are able to not only suppress the light of truth but also create an alternate version of it. Thankfully, democracies have repeatedly proven that societies aren't bound to obey the Newtonian laws of physics, as long as the people maintain our collective hope and the unified will to oppose inertia.

But when inertia replaces the free will to resist it—when voting, activism, and advocacy cease to matter in the mind of the citizens—nihilistic autocrats win more of the only thing they hold sacred: power. Russia, China, and North Korea are not bizarre outliers where democracy is either strangled or in full retreat. The same ideology and forces controlling those totalitarian regimes continue to win victories elsewhere, in places like Hungary and Venezuela. Furthermore, while unthinkable only a generation or two ago, decades of nihilistic greed and civic inertia ushered in a degree of political corruption, dark-money funding, and collective disregard for the rule of law that has America situated before a totalitarian abyss, as if she were a comatose cliff diver. If a critical mass of us awakens, even if the awakening is in the middle of free fall, maybe we can prevent catastrophe.

The enemy of would-be totalitarians is truth; their survival depends on creating a warped version of it with an ever-present, and often explicit, goal of cementing themselves in power. Not even the light of truth can escape the geopolitical black hole of a totalitarian regime, so democracy truly does "die in darkness."[38] To discover truth, speak it, and preserve it is to wage war against the inertia that totalitarianism depends upon. Recall from the opening chapter that life opposes inertia. This allows us to confidently assert that democracy is both the life and light that we achieve through the collective strength and will of the people. The true power in democracy must be shared among many instead of consolidated by a few; this fact simultaneously explains the definition, purpose, and infinite nature of democracy. Democracy is undoubtedly an eternal cause that depends upon the will of successive generations to sustain it. In an era when truth, light, life, and democracy are fading, it comforts me to recall the smiling three-month-old baby girl from a previous chapter. Truth and democracy may suffer assaults and setbacks, but the causes are eternal. As long as human life on Earth exists, truth and democracy will never suffer their final defeats. As long as humanity exists, hope will exist with it; millions of years of evolution have baked hope into our DNA. Even the most robust empires in history dissolved after a few centuries. No modern tyrannical regime stands a chance to undo the hope of humanity in a couple of decades. Is it clear yet that the causes of truth seekers and democracy lovers are undeniably eternal?

While democracy has proven challenging and messy for us to maintain and build upon, our ability to see beauty in that mess isn't just crucial—it's existential. If we, the people, don't love democracy, if we lack the strength and will to protect, preserve, and keep it, then power and inertia are guaranteed to take it away from us. If or when that happens, no election can bring our democracy back. While there are plenty of examples of citizens voting democracy out, not once in history has a nation been able to vote a democracy in without first overthrowing a foreign conqueror, authoritarian regime, or royal family.

Chapter 10

HUMOR

Eat, drink, and be merry,
for tomorrow, we die.
—Kurt Vonnegut, *Cat's Cradle*

Hey, careful man!
There's a beverage here!
—The Dude, *The Big Lebowski*

THINGS GOT PRETTY HEAVY IN the last chapter, so this seems like a perfect spot to lighten the mood with a riff on humor. My first paid writing job was creating satire for a website that resembles a medical version of *The Onion*. I earned fifty bucks for every article that ran online. This side gig wasn't exactly enough to keep the lights on, but it served as a nice outlet for the deepening cynicism I was developing over my years in the ER. I quietly enjoyed the anonymity of a pseudonym. My most popular story was about a hospital administrator intervening during a cardiac arrest on a commercial flight. Since he was of no use in the medical sense, he sprang into action, handing out satisfaction surveys to each passenger before the diverted flight landed. Absurdities abound in our modern world; satire is really just the art of holding lenses and mirrors up to those absurdities.

It's fitting that *human* and *humor* are such similar words, since humor is an incredible gift to humanity. Understanding the human condition builds the foundation for our sense of humor. We know that none of us will get out of here alive, so we might as well connect, laugh, and enjoy each other's company in the time we do have. When I reflect on the people I've come across who have magnetic, charismatic senses of humor, I always think of my mom's brother, Tom. You'll remember from a prior chapter that my Uncle Tom Mustard is a retired Episcopal priest. The more stories I hear about Uncle Tom, the more it seems that he has managed to pack the experiences of six or ten lifetimes into his single one.

My mom's family grew up on a farm in Southwest Virginia. She and her five siblings have madcap stories from their younger years on that farm. The kids worked in the fields, hiked in the woods, and played in the creeks surrounding it. My mom told a story of how she carried a broken arm around for a few weeks without telling her parents; she had injured it after falling off a vine in the woods that she wasn't supposed to be swinging on. Once, to win a bet, my mom's oldest brother, Eddie, rolled up an entire angel food cake their mom had baked and stuffed it into his pants pocket. Even though he knew he'd have to deal with his dad's belt later, he really wanted to prove himself and win that bet. Uncle Tom was a hell-raiser growing up; he was also a Renaissance man long before anyone realized that Renaissance men were a dying breed. He could sing, dance, shoot a rifle, win fistfights, excel at sports, and chase girls; it seems he was good at just about anything he decided to do.

For a couple of summers, he played Johnse Hatfield in *Hatfield and McCoy* at a well-known and popular outdoor theater. If you haven't heard of it, *Hatfield and McCoy* is a play by Shawn Pfautsch about a real post–Civil War family feud along the West Virginia–Kentucky border. Johnse is the lead character, a dashing and charismatic prankster whom Uncle Tom was born to play. My mom had at least a dozen stories about Uncle Tom's hot temper and abundant charm. Our family thinks that maybe God "scared him straight" one summer when he was a teenager and got struck by lightning. His eardrums ruptured, and he was essentially deaf for a few weeks after that. These days, everyone agrees that Uncle Tom has mellowed with age; whether the lightning strike was the cause or just a coincidence is still up for debate.

Both of my mom's parents died when she and her siblings were young. Her dad had a heart attack at age forty-six, and her mom passed away a couple years later from surgical complications related to a brain tumor. The eldest siblings had to grow up quickly and live nearly independently, while the younger ones went to live with aunts and uncles on neighboring farms. Through these experiences, my mom developed a "life goes on" mentality. "When something disappointing or sad happens, you have the choice of whether to laugh or cry," she advised me once. Most often, she laughed. It seems ironic, but people who suffer trauma and loss at a young age often develop an incredibly refreshing sense of humor. The Mustard siblings are proof of that fact. My mom's family is full of practical jokers and raunchy comedians who refuse to take themselves seriously. Reunions and holiday get-togethers are always rowdy affairs where siblings and cousins sing around the piano, play backyard football or pitch horseshoes, eat potluck, shoot pool, and laugh until we cry.

Since Uncle Tom is the family chaplain, he always says the blessing before we eat and officiates our weddings and funerals. While he can be serious and somber when the situation demands, I am often amazed at the way he can effortlessly lighten everyone's mood with humor. On more than one occasion, I've heard him tell stories during eulogies that make brand-new widows and widowers belly laugh. My Aunt Sue lost her husband (who was coincidentally also named Tom) over twenty years ago. He was an ebullient, bald, and burly guy who had never met a stranger in his life. In a remote accident, he had lost the fourth and fifth fingers of his right hand. Pretty early into the eulogy, Uncle Tom mentioned Uncle-in-law Tom's exuberant and intense three-fingered handshake, and the parlor of the funeral home burst into laughter. I remember watching my Aunt Sue smile and chuckle as she wiped tears from her eyes. Miraculously,

Uncle Tom's humor never feels out of place; it hits in a timely way and always lands perfectly. He has a unique ability to unfailingly connect with anyone, especially people who are hurting. I think the emotional trauma he suffered as a young man helped create in him an uncommon empathy that grieving people sense almost instantly. Connecting with a devastated person and reminding them that they still know how to laugh is probably worth a dozen therapy sessions.

Since it would be a crime to write a chapter on humor and not include a single joke, I'm going to borrow this one that I remember Uncle Tom telling at a wedding reception:

A team of scientists and psychologists start a study on differences between optimists and pessimists. They decide to create two separate rooms with a wall of one-way observation glass in their lab. One room is filled with toys and games like air hockey, pop-a-shot basketball, darts, and a pool table. There's a huge TV with cable and a video game console hooked up to it with at least two dozen popular video games. Comfortable chairs and couches line the walls. There are bowls of snacks and a mini fridge stocked with soda pop and chocolate milk. The other room is filled with nothing but horse manure piled three feet deep.

To start the study, one of the scientists escorts a pessimistic twelve-year-old into the room with games, snacks, and the huge TV. The scientist tells the kid that he can stay in the room as long as he wants; when he wants out, all he has to do is push a button by the door, and it will open. The scientist walks out, and the door closes. The kid looks around and then shoots pool for a couple of minutes and then throws a dozen or so darts at the dartboard. After that, the scientists watch as he grabs a handful of chips, cracks open a soda pop, and plops on the couch to play video games. He cycles through three-to-four games in about twenty minutes, lets out a loud sigh, walks to the door, and pushes the button. It opens, and a scientist asks why he was ready to come out so soon.

"I was getting bored. There just wasn't anything fun to do in there."

"How long did he last?" one psychologist asks another.

The second scientist glances at the stopwatch and replies, "Twenty-four minutes and thirty-eight seconds."

The scientist with the stopwatch scrawls the time into her data table, and the team moves on to the next kid, whom earlier testing has labeled as an eternal optimist. The optimistic twelve-year-old is led into the room filled with horse manure and is given the same instructions. Stay as long as you want; all you have to do is hit the button, and the door will open. The scientists' jaws drop as they watch the optimistic kid enter a fit of giddiness. He starts wading through the manure, scooping it with both hands and throwing it all over the room. He crisscrosses the room from corner to corner, scooping the horse manure in front of him to clear a somewhat walkable path; then he starts to move in rows, back and forth like someone pushing a lawn mower, scooping and throwing the manure as he goes.

Finally, one of the awestruck scientists is able to speak. He holds down the button to the intercom into the kid's room. "Why are you so excited to be in a room filled with horse manure?" he asks.

Grinning ear to ear, the optimistic kid replies, "With all this horse shit, there's GOTTA be a pony in here somewhere!"

Uncle Tom is the unwavering optimist in the joke. He knows that, in many of life's situations, there's no pony, only shit. But he understands the joy that comes in searching for that pony; even if we never find the pony, the search itself can create and multiply joy. Soul-sucking nihilists repeatedly tell us that optimism is useless. But if optimism can conjure up infectious joy where there previously was none, then the nihilists are the ones who are full of shit. Optimism is one of the most useful tools humanity has.

Chapter 11

MOTIVATION

Someday soon, perhaps in forty years, there will be no one
alive who has ever known me. That's when I will be truly
dead—when I exist in no one's memory. I thought a lot about
how someone very old is the last living individual to have known
some person or cluster of people. When that person dies, the whole
cluster dies, too, vanishes from the living memory. I wonder who
that person will be for me. Whose death will make me truly dead?
—Irvin D. Yalom, *Love's Executioner and Other Tales of Psychotherapy*

For what shall it profit a man, if he shall gain the
whole world, and lose his own soul?
—Mark 8:36 (KJV)

YOU'RE HOLDING THIS BOOK IN your hands because I am afraid. As we age, the certainty of mortality begins to settle in; we start to become preoccupied with the question of what follows death. When I was only twenty-two, my mom died suddenly. It was September, and I wasn't with her since it was about two weeks into my first year of medical school. In retrospect, I can't retrace my timeline of navigating the five stages of grief, but I do remember that, after the shock and disbelief subsided, I found myself facing an important decision. Would I take a year off and restart school the following fall, or would I, wounded and demoralized, attempt to rally and make up one of the most challenging weeks of anatomy and physiology? I couldn't begin to envision what I would do for an entire year away from school. I worried that staying home might derail my plans and keep me from achieving my goal of becoming a doctor. So I went back to school and got to work on a brutal few weeks of lectures and lab sessions.

During one of these make-up sessions, an assistant anatomy professor took me aside, looked me in the eyes, and said, "You know something? You've got the heart of a lion." It was incredible how seen and validated that statement made me feel. Buehner's words from a couple chapters back ring true for me; I have never forgotten that feeling of being seen. I believe part of my identity was forged in that moment. I liked being described as resilient, gritty, focused, and tough; increasingly, I began to behave like someone who was born with those traits. Most of us underestimate the impact we can have on young minds—this is misguided. We mustn't neglect our own power to encourage young people and articulate the strengths we see in them. Today, I can trace much of who I am and how I view myself back to a professor's comment that took about five seconds for him to share.

Psychologists have long used the sensitivity to reward and punishment to explain human behaviors and behavioral patterns. Humans feel varying degrees of sensitivity to rewards and punishments.[39] Speaking generally, those of us who are more sensitive to rewards are more likely to be spontaneous and engage in riskier behaviors, while those of us who are more sensitive to punishment tend to be more subdued and cautious. Yet ultimately, all humans seek to stimulate a universal reward pathway in the brain. This complex structure is known as the mesolimbic system, and its central chemical neurotransmitter is dopamine. Behaviors that dump dopamine into this pathway are literally addictive—we will perform them repeatedly to achieve the rush of instinctive joy this neurologic pathway brings. Dozens of both healthy and maladaptive behaviors predictably activate the brain's reward system, including food, sex, alcohol, gambling, exercise, and the use of smartphones.[40]

We do not yet fully understand the neuroanatomic machinery that determines how punishment impacts behavior. Like cousins, the avoidance of punishment and emotion of fear appear related, but still distinct. By this, I mean that our behavior can be motivated by an awareness of the possibility of a negative feeling or future result, even when we do not feel afraid.[41] A couple of times a week, my dog and I run past a yard with two vocal and menacing German shepherds. Thankfully, an invisible electric fence marks boundaries that the shepherds have learned to respect. It isn't fear of the shock that prevents them from charging at us; they've merely learned how to avoid punishment by accepting the boundary. Importantly, punishment doesn't necessarily involve physical pain. The potential for embarrassment, public failure, rejection, and criticism exerts enormous influence on human behavior too. Once we learn that we can avoid negative feedback and emotions by respecting others' boundaries and asserting our own, we don't need to be afraid. But while avoiding challenging emotions entirely can provide an effective way for humans to dodge fear, the strategy is an unhealthy one in the long term.

With this neurobiology in mind, I'm compelled to discuss the developed world's smartphone addiction. I can easily see why humans are predisposed to languish on social media or binge TikTok videos for hours at a time, since these devices enable us to continuously stoke our dopamine reward pathways with no real risk of public failure, pain, or rejection. The private rewards that social media brings are pretty minor. Having a laugh at a funny cat video or receiving a "like" from afar doesn't bring joy or acceptance equivalent to the social rewards of winning a basketball championship with a real-life team. But someone on the couch watching videos and reels has no concern that they may fail, so the reward-to-punishment ratio is infinite. This is the inertia that totalitarian regimes feed upon. In a totalitarian's ideal society, every potential dissenting citizen would spend their free time melting into a couch while fixated on a two-dimensional screen. Humans in the smartphone era can now experience an endless deluge of tiny rewards without any risk of punishment and the negative feelings it evokes in us. The main reason why almost everyone in the developed world is addicted to smartphones is that millions of years of evolutionary biology guaranteed that we would become addicted to them.

If we define anxiety as an irrational fear, then clearly smartphones have played a significant role in creating the anxiety epidemic and our modern culture of fear. Avoidance does not conquer anxiety, but rather perpetuates it. Smartphones encourage and enable our avoidance of fear-inducing and potentially uncomfortable social situations. But a person compulsively scrolling social media while stapled to a couch is not really living; they're forfeiting their life to inertia. Trading face-to-face interaction for virtual socializing is choosing a fickle, less-meaningful substitute that won't fulfill the deep need for connection with other humans. Far too many centuries of evolutionary neuro-programming have passed for humans to suddenly switch into lives of only virtual connections. As with other addictions, the only way to release the grip of smartphones and social media is with a sequence of acknowledgment, intention, and will. Some of the students I've advised adopted a study strategy I suggest often: switch the phone to Airplane Mode and set a thirty-minute timer. Then put the phone on the other side of the room. Focus and study for those thirty minutes, then go check what you've missed when the timer goes off. One of these students later remarked that this strategy enabled them to accomplish two hours of studying in thirty minutes. This student discovered willpower. Willpower in the face of addiction is the theme of my next chapter.

At the beginning of this chapter, I said that you're holding this book in your hands because I'm afraid. My biggest fear is that I will be forgotten after I die. I guess it's either morbid or a sign of emotional maturity that I've accepted the certainty of death. One of my teaching colleagues and I have an uncanny knack for getting deeply philosophical in even the shortest of conversations. Ann is a fun-loving mom and math teacher with about forty years of experience. She loves to travel and doesn't take herself too seriously. She's an ultimate professional driven by a sense of duty and purpose, but she never seems hurried. A conversation with Ann makes me feel as though she has all the time in the world—time to pause and reflect, time for a funny story, and time to travel along a tangent and look up a recipe that was a big hit. I think we connect because we're able to keep our sense of humor while openly acknowledging that no one gets out of here alive. I told her about my fear of dying and being forgotten.

"You know," Ann said, "my Jewish mom says that we all have two deaths. The first one is the death of the body, and the second one is the death of the soul. She says the soul dies when no one who is living remembers you anymore."

I guess I'm kind of ashamed that this book is more a product of my fear than my motivation to achieve. Numerous relatives of mine never made it into their fifties or sixties; I'm approaching fifty myself. My own mom only made it to fifty-one. That reality sometimes hits me like a splash of ice water on my face. What if I don't have any more than a few years to create something meaningful to leave behind? It's a little disappointing to know that fear still motivates me as much as it did when I was decades younger, but I imagine I can view the book as an accomplishment, independent of the inspirations and motivations behind it. Writing it has brought a sense of peace in the knowledge that, at the very least, I will leave something behind besides a corpse and a trust fund. The motivation to leave the tangible artifact you're holding in your hands compelled me to eschew a comfortable, easy state of inertia. Most certainly, there are people in power who are uncomfortable with the ideas presented here, but aren't these the exact ideas that are most needed if we are to live and resist inertia?

Chapter 12
WILLPOWER

Willpower gets you started.
Habits get you results.
—Priit Kallas

It's hard to beat a person who never gives up.
—Babe Ruth

IN A LONG PHASE OF my twenties and thirties, I was more deeply immersed in fitness culture than I am now. I lifted weights three or four times per week, ran half-marathons, did a mini triathlon, worked out at a boxing gym, and enjoyed adventure obstacle races. I still love to exercise, but I have to admit that being an endurance athlete isn't as significant a piece of my identity as it once was. Although I don't recall the source of the quote, I remember that during this era of my peak physical fitness, I internalized the assertion that "there's no such thing as willpower, only the desire to make a change." The statement had a self-determining dose of agency buried in it that served as motivation for me in those years.

Back in the 1990s, people tended to view willpower as a gene in their DNA that they either had a copy of or didn't. I rejected that notion, and therefore the term *willpower*. I viewed challenges as matters of choice, tests of internal fortitude that I could decide to pass or fail. It now seems that most of society agrees that while our choices can be influenced by our individual genetic makeup, they depend on many more factors than that. In light of this, I've gone back to freely using the term *willpower*. Ultimately, the pragmatist in me understands that naming a behavior is purely semantic; actions and results are what matter. The American Psychological Association defines willpower as "the ability to delay gratification, resisting short-term temptations in order to meet long-term goals."[42]

Anyone who reads the news or stops to examine their own personal relationships receives frequent reminders that addictions are difficult, and sometimes impossible, to break. The neurological reward pathways I described in the previous chapter remain potent determinants of our behaviors. Can we humans resist these powerful forces within us? Thankfully, we can. The key to overcoming our preprogrammed behavioral patterns is pausing to examine our own identities before we act on impulse. As is the case in determining our purposes, we make more conscious decisions only after firmly establishing our identities. Additionally, while it may seem obvious, it's important to recognize that the ability to make conscious choices about our behaviors arises from belief in free will. No nihilist in history has ever broken an addiction without someone else forcing them to break it.

Alcoholism is a recurring challenge in my family, particularly on my mom's side. Two of her brothers battled it. One defeated it; the other was felled by it. Uncle Tom is the one who got sober. These two uncles aren't my only family members who have struggled with alcohol addiction. I sat down with my cousin, Sarah, to learn more about her experience. Uncle Tom's granddaughter, Sarah is a teacher, coach, and mom who is a few years younger than me. Unfortunately, she inherited a predisposition for alcoholism from both of her parents. Sarah has been sober now for over three years, and has successfully rebuilt her life after it all came crashing down.

In high school, Sarah was incredibly bright, driven, and goal oriented. She didn't make B's—ever. At age fifteen, she had her first couple of drinks.

"Do you remember how you felt then?" I asked early on in our recent conversation.

"I knew immediately that I would do it again. I liked the way it made me feel. Back then, I often wondered if I was going to implode or explode. I was constantly stressed out, and the stress disappeared after those drinks."

Sarah was, and still is, an incredibly high achiever. She committed to academic and athletic success early and earned top honors in her high school class. On quite a few occasions over her high school years, drinking provided a welcome off-ramp from the infinite interstate of boundless achievement and unrelenting pressure. She was accepted to her college of choice, where alcohol became more than a stress reliever; binge drinking became a habit.

"When I got to college, the rules and norms about alcohol became more fuzzy and obscure. I couldn't control my drinking pace. I'd get stumbling drunk at football tailgates and blackout drunk at parties. I remember going to a tailgate with a friend who couldn't attend the game later because she was booked to babysit that afternoon. She had one beer from the keg and then cut herself off. That level of restraint was totally foreign to me; I never stopped at one drink. That Saturday afternoon, I understood for the first time that I had a problem."

In graduate school, Sarah's alcohol addiction further tightened its grip. "I began to obsess about drinking. I made some rules about when I could drink and when I couldn't. If I had a day off, I would down a couple of drinks and then go run errands. It wasn't long until, most nights, I was drinking to the point of blacking out. When the COVID pandemic hit in March of 2020, the lockdown removed the rules I'd made for myself. I started drinking earlier in the day since there was nowhere to go. By then I was married, and one afternoon, my husband and I sat down to discuss our drinking habits and patterns. He and I both made a conscious, verbal agreement to cut back. He did so pretty easily. The addiction had taken too firm a hold for me, I guess; I started concealing things and drinking in secret."

SARAH DESCRIBED HER SHELL GAME of hiding wine and liquor bottles around in closets, the laundry room, and the garage. She learned that a tank of gas cost about exactly the same as two bottles of gas station wine, so the credit card statement aligned perfectly when she lied about filling up her car. About a year after the pandemic struck the US, Sarah got a wake-up call. She got into the shower drunk and passed out, striking her forehead and brow on a shower fixture. Inebriated, concussed, and pouring blood from her face, her husband drove her to the ER. The staff took her in, and a doctor examined her and sewed up her eyebrow laceration. Amazingly to her, no one at the hospital asked her about alcohol, even though she was certain that she reeked of it. She was relieved that she didn't hurt herself worse, but more relieved to avoid the shame of being found out. Leaving the hospital with fresh stitches and bandages, she interpreted the misadventure as a close call.

"I've got to give it up, at least for a while," she told herself. "I'm on a really dangerous path." When she got home, she committed to abstaining for at least the next week.

The next evening, Sarah and her husband attended a backyard cookout in their neighborhood. She was bruised and bandaged from the previous evening's escapade and had to recount the story of her injury at least a half-dozen times. She spotted a cooler full of beer, and before long, she gave in to her anxiety and craving for alcohol. The promise she had made to dry out didn't last a single day. She felt trapped. *You're fucked*, she thought to herself as she slurped down her second beer of the evening. Sheer will and internal promises weren't going to rid her of her alcohol addiction.

"I started talking to Opa"—Sarah's grandad, my Uncle Tom—"and mom about my problem because I knew they had both been there. I went to some meetings. For the first dozen or so meetings, I was one of those people who barely spoke and darted out the door as soon as it was over. I remember thinking that the other alcoholics there were in far worse shape than I was. They would tell stories of fights, arrests, and how they'd alienated their own families. I felt sorry for them, sure, but I also took some comfort in the fact that I wasn't in the same terrible shape that they were. 'These people aren't like me,' I told myself. I didn't have the foresight then to recognize that their stories were foreshadowing what I would experience myself if I didn't quit drinking."

Later that summer, Sarah had what she recognized as her first episode of alcohol withdrawal. She had stopped drinking daily, but stringing together multiple days of sobriety felt impossible thanks to the tremors, sweats, and sense of impending doom that accompanied them. She made the decision to enter inpatient treatment. Upon her release, she remained sober for about two weeks before suffering a relapse. In retrospect, this relapse served as the wake-up call that Sarah needed. When she regained her senses, she was in police custody and learned that she'd drunk herself to an alcohol level of 0.35 and crashed her car into a tree. She had arrived at the bottom.

"Miraculously, I hadn't hurt or killed anyone," she recalled. "I had an immediate change in my psyche after the crash and arrest. I realized that I would die young and possibly kill someone else if I didn't stop drinking. I had become one of the people at the meetings who I believed was in far worse shape than me. Alcohol had become my only coping mechanism, and I was going to change that."

Sarah committed to her sobriety program and began to contribute more enthusiastically. The cravings became far less strong; she could overcome them with intentional decisions and a support system of people she could reach out to during tempting or stressful times.

"Without question, the program is the reason I've stayed sober," Sarah related during our interview. "There are still occasional cravings and plenty of stressful situations, but my instinct to pour a drink has been replaced by an instinct to call my sponsor, my Opa, or my mom. Connecting with them serves to 'pump the brakes' and allows me to make more conscious, less-impulsive decisions."

In addition to the physical scars, her addiction also left some invisible ones. Years of alcoholism washed away the bonds of her first marriage, which ended in divorce; her kids now split their time between her and their dad. And sobriety hasn't magically solved all her problems or prevented new tragedies from finding her. After years of illness, pain, and addiction of his own, Sarah's father took his own life. Sarah knows that new stressful challenges, grief, regret, and angst could compel her to start drinking again if she doesn't remain vigilant and connected to her identity and community. She found that connecting to a community of relatives and peers lessened her shame at first and completely eradicated it over time.

"Drinking alone because you're addicted and ashamed is probably the unhealthiest coping mechanism someone can develop, and that's exactly where I was, a place where my disease and its only cure were the same thing—more alcohol," Sarah related to me in a follow-up interview. "It was a self-perpetuating spin cycle into an abyss. But the connections I made with others in my program and family members who'd been where I was removed the shame I felt. When I need reassurance or encouragement, there are almost a dozen people I can reach out to who won't judge me. Just knowing those connections are there is almost as comforting as the relief I feel when I need to activate them."

Since her new husband and her kids now attend Al-Anon and Alateen sessions that often run concurrently with Sarah's scheduled group meetings, she's been able to strengthen connections with family members who haven't necessarily been to the same dark places she has. While willpower may be an internal force, it's certainly bolstered by external human connections.

When I spoke with Sarah, I shared my ideas on willpower and described how they've changed over the years. "After almost half a century, I've come to define willpower as a conscious, intentional bet on your future self, a bet that tomorrow's you will be better than today's."

"I agree completely, Keith. I do," she responded. "A bet begins with belief. And no one places a bet they don't believe they can win. To exercise willpower is to prove to yourself that you're worthy of believing in—believing that you're a worthy cause."

Damn. If that's not a powerful call to recognize the agency we have in our own lives, then I don't know what is. I'm not advocating or encouraging gambling here; I'm merely stating that a bet on yourself is a bet that you can literally *will* into fruition. Las Vegas has thousands of gaming tables, but not a single one of them offers that.

Recently, Sarah reached the three-year mark of her sober journey. With each passing day, her recovery connections and willpower tame the forces of addiction and impulse. To me, Sarah's story is a reminder that a hero is really just a regular person who has firmly established their identity, then used that identity as a touchstone to make intentional and conscious decisions. Stories like hers are collisions of neuroscience and poetry. They serve to illustrate that when we combine free will with belief in ourselves, we humans become empowered with the force we need to overcome inertia and inspire others to action.

Chapter 13

CONFIDENCE

Our doubts are traitors,
And make us lose the good we oft might win,
By fearing to attempt.
—Shakespeare, *Measure for Measure*

When the shit goes down,
you better be ready.
—Cypress Hill, *When the Shit Goes Down*

I'M STILL NOT SURE IF this chapter should be called "confidence" or "competence." Initially, those words may sound like neighboring branches on the same tree, but I think they are farther apart than that. Maybe they are more like branches of different trees in the same forest. I view competence as an external measure of aptitude as assessed by others who work in the same field or share the same hobby. Confidence, on the other hand, is someone's perception of their own competence. When someone senses their own competence, they automatically feel a degree of confidence.

Discordance arises when someone feels confident, while those around them see incompetence; each of us is familiar with at least a few people who are rather confident but deficient in competence. Due to human gullibility, bias, and greed, "style over substance" personalities commonly ascend to fame, notoriety, and power. Country people know this as the "all hat, no cattle" phenomenon. The bluster, exaggerations, and carefully crafted persona of an incompetent but ambitious person compels some observers to focus on their impressive metaphorical cowboy hat while ignoring the fact that they don't have much underneath it. Near the other end of the spectrum, those of us with impostor syndrome gain confidence slowly, even after we have developed a solid foundation of competence.

I imagine most of us have heard of the Dunning–Kruger effect, traditionally known as the tendency for novices in a particular field to experience a phase of master-level confidence once they have developed entry-level competence. Consider the example of the first-semester psychology student who confidently assigns psychiatric diagnoses to dozens of friends and family members. However, some debate now stirs on what Dunning and Kruger actually discovered in their studies. One widely accepted argument asserts that the Dunning–Kruger effect is the tendency of most people to believe that they perform better than average, even though it's mathematically impossible for the majority of people to be above average.[43]

I think most of us agree that in an ideal scenario, competence develops before confidence. A supremely confident but minimally competent employee, student, or doctor is at best a liability and at worst a threat to life and limb. But what about the reverse? Can perfectly competent executives, cops, or doctors who lack sufficient confidence become harmful or dangerous as well? I think so. Highly competent people who lack confidence are prone to overthinking and analysis paralysis. Making timely decisions with limited information and executing rapid interventions are essential skills for people who work in conditions of urgency—people like police, military and government leaders, and emergency physicians.

In the spring of my year as chief resident in emergency medicine, an EMS crew rolled in with a drowsy, poorly responsive man who appeared to be in his late fifties. The crew had been dispatched to the airport to pick up this patient, whom bystanders had seen pass out. He still had not returned to normal consciousness. We had no information about him other than what was on his driver's license and plane ticket; we knew nothing about his medical history or medications. He groaned occasionally when we shouted questions at him, and he withdrew all four of his limbs equally from a painful stimulus, which argued against a major stroke. In the ambulance, he had shown no response to the opioid antidote. His blood sugar was normal. His blood pressure, however, was not. It was about 75/40—dangerously low.

Cases like this are fairly common in busy emergency departments. They present often enough that my attending physician on duty was busy evaluating a different but equally ill patient. Clearly, I would be the doctor in charge of this case. At that point in my training, I had already treated dozens, if not hundreds, of patients in shock without clear causes, so I was confident in my ability to care for the patient in front of me. I knew he was in the transition between life and death—recall the definition of *shock* from the first chapter. In cases like these, emergency medical teams follow a set of basic interventions and diagnostics like an algorithm; a systematic approach is most likely to bring a favorable outcome.

I looked at the patient's EKG (heart tracing), which showed a normal heart rate and rhythm and no sign of a large-vessel heart attack. The paramedics had placed an IV in each of the patient's arms and were infusing fluids without any change in his blood pressure or level of responsiveness. The list of potential problems was long, including conditions such as a leaking aneurysm of the aorta, meningitis, massive bleeding from a stomach ulcer, an overdose, and a raging bloodstream infection. I took a quick look at his heart and aorta with a bedside ultrasound—no obvious aneurysm, and no significant fluid around the heart. This patient needed a slew of blood tests and some advanced CT imaging for our team to figure out why he was in a death spiral.

When a patient is in critical condition, securing their airway early is important. Recall from the opening chapter on life that a constant supply of oxygen is necessary for cells to survive, make energy, and perform their respective functions. A reliable pathway to pump adequate amounts of oxygen into the lungs can be the difference between life and death. So we prepared to intubate, which means inserting a breathing tube through the patient's mouth and into his windpipe, to provide that pathway.

A doctor intubating a deteriorating patient is akin to a pilot pulling the stick back and lifting the nose of a speeding plane off the runway at takeoff. We have at least a dozen boxes to check in preparation for that moment. Once the pilot has made the decision to lift off the ground, the plane *has to* fly—it's non-negotiable at that point. Systematic preparation ensures that it will. In the handful of minutes before intubation, we had our patient breathe the highest concentration of oxygen available through a mask; this allowed some wiggle room on time in case I had trouble finessing the tube into the right spot. Typically, pushing a quick sequence of medications through the IV renders a patient unconscious and unable to move so that passing the tube through the vocal cords becomes easier for the doctor and painless for the patient. We had already drawn up this combination of medications. I surveyed the resuscitation room and equipment nearby; the staff stood ready, awaiting my word to inject the medications through the IV and into the patient. Before giving the okay to our bedside nurse to push the strong sedative and muscle-paralyzing medication, I glanced up at the cardiac monitor above the patient.

"Wait," I said. "Something isn't right. His T waves look pretty generous. I think they are abnormal." A particular segment of the EKG tracing gives clues about potassium levels in a patient's blood serum. The look of our patient's tracing had set off an alarm bell in my mind.

"Does that matter right now?" the lead nurse responded.

"It does if his potassium is high," I answered. "Let's get a STAT set of electrolytes to make sure before we push the drugs."

This test was crucial because patients with high potassium levels can't tolerate one of the medications in the combination for intubation—it drives their potassium up further. This difference is of little consequence in a patient with a normal serum potassium level, but it can be enough to kill a patient whose potassium is already elevated. High potassium levels are toxic to the heart's ability to function, decreasing pumping ability and causing fatal heart rhythms. We held back the drugs and continued infusing saline into the patient's veins while the respiratory therapist ran the bedside electrolyte panel.

"Potassium is 8.7," she informed us.

It was a terribly high level, one that would require multiple treatments, including dialysis, before the patient suffered cardiovascular collapse. When we gave our patient the standard sequence of treatments to drive circulating potassium out of his blood and into his body's tissues, his blood pressure improved, and he began to speak more coherently. As lab values and imaging results returned over the next couple of hours, we learned that he had developed acute kidney failure due to total obstruction of urine flow out of his bladder. His prostate had evidently been ballooning over the previous weeks and, eventually, had blocked all urine flow out. Since excess potassium must be eliminated by the kidneys into the urine, the blockage had caused our patient's potassium to slowly build up to a near-fatal level. He just happened to be waiting on a connecting flight at our city's airport when everything came crashing down. A few years before, I'd sworn an oath to help and serve the sick and injured. On that day, competence and doubt prevented me from accidentally nudging a desperately sick person over the edge of a cliff. If I hadn't doubted, if I had been overconfident and cavalier, that's exactly what would have happened.

At other moments in the ER, hesitation is the enemy. When a case requires decisive action, excessive doubt can harm patients. I was at least six-to-eight years out of residency and into my career as an emergency physician when I performed my first and only cricothyrotomy. In crude terms, a cricothyrotomy means cutting a hole in the front of a patient's neck to insert a breathing tube directly into their windpipe, bypassing their mouth and throat. This procedure isn't necessary very often, but every emergency medicine and anesthesia resident practices it a few times on mannequins or sheep tracheas. In inexperienced hands, a scalpel to the neck can not only fail to secure an airway, but also destroy arteries, veins, and nerves. So a medical resident needs several teaching and practice sessions to learn how to perform the procedure correctly. A cricothyrotomy isn't a casual, elective procedure; it's imperative to do it quickly and correctly, or the patient will die.

The ER staff and I were scrambling through a typically boisterous Friday night when an EMS crew brought in a twenty-something man who had been stabbed in the right side of the neck with a steak knife. He was sitting upright, answering in hushed tones, and looking terrified. The trauma surgeon and anesthesiologist were twenty-to-thirty minutes away, and this patient needed a definitive airway before they arrived. I knew there was a good chance the anatomy of his neck and throat was already distorted, so we prepared for cricothyrotomy in case the old-fashioned way of intubating the patient wasn't possible.

After we had pushed the intubation drugs, I looked down his throat with a scope and saw no reliable anatomy. The patient already had a sizable neck hematoma (a collection of blood) pushing his neck structures to the left and out of my view. This was not a time for hubris or pride; my fellow doctor on duty that night was more experienced than I was, so I asked him to take a look as well. His observations were the same as mine. In the anesthesia vernacular, we were now dealing with a failed airway. I can't really describe the mode I shifted into at that point except to say that it was an odd combination of feeling incredibly distant, yet also hyperaware. After our team had stabilized the patient, and he had been whisked away to the operating room, we had a minute to debrief. The lead nurse approached, her hand raised for a high five.

"Wow, great work! You know it took you less than two minutes from making the incision to sewing stitches on a tube in his trachea?"

I realized then that I had lost all concept of time. She could have told me it had taken me fifteen seconds or fifteen minutes, and I would have believed her. I've read stories of soldiers and police experiencing dire situations and later recounting that, during those moments of extreme stress, their "training took over." Looking back on my experience with this patient, that's the feeling I felt—almost as if I wasn't the person who performed the procedure. I felt more as if I'd watched myself do it. We later found out that the stab wound had punctured our patient's jugular vein and carotid artery. He had a couple of surgeries and spent a few days in the ICU, but ultimately walked out of the hospital. I had carried out a successful emergency cricothyrotomy on a real patient for the first time. That night, I had just enough doubt in my ability to perform a standard intubation to prepare for an exceedingly rare emergency procedure, and just enough confidence to execute it.

I don't have any flowery wisdom on how to achieve the proper balance of confidence and competence. While there's no such thing as an excess of competence, it's clear that, depending on the circumstances, we can harm people with both overconfidence and a lack of confidence. Meanwhile, those with enough self-awareness to match their level of confidence to their level of competence can become valuable assets to any group or organization. When a new hire or team member arrives humble and curious, more experienced teammates typically award them a bevy of opportunities to learn skills and solve problems. That newbie is virtually guaranteed to develop competence. I've been there, and it's true. When that newly competent addition is immersed in a culture of encouragement and trust, they'll begin to develop as a leader. I've been there too.

I had the good fortune to train under an emergency physician named John Marx. While I don't expect that his name will ring a bell with most readers, the man is a legend in the emergency medicine community. John was a leader in the field for decades before I even began my residency training. What I remember most about him was his striking combination of intellectual brilliance and personal humility. At first, it seemed like an act. But within a couple hours of working alongside him, the genuine nature of his character became inarguably obvious.

I remember one of the first shifts we worked together during my intern year. The ER was bursting at the seams with patients; we must have had forty-to-fifty people in the waiting room. I had just seen an affable thirty-something New York native who had gotten his big toe crushed while he was trying to move a piano. He wasn't bleeding all that much, but a pretty large purple collection of blood had built up under his toenail, and his whole toe was exquisitely tender to touch. I knew he needed some X-rays but wondered if I needed to remove the toenail to check for a nasty injury to the nail bed underneath. So I went to ask John for advice. Some supervising doctors would sigh and roll their eyes at this request—it was a toe injury in a sea of many more ill and injured patients. Yet John paused what he was working on and patiently listened while I recounted my patient's presentation. Then a smirk came across his face, leaving me to wonder what he found funny as we walked together to my patient's room to have a look at his toe.

John introduced himself to the patient with a smile and handshake, first establishing their connection as New Yorkers. He then began to ask questions about the specifications of the piano that had caused the injury. It seemed a bit strange that John cared so much about the heavy blunt object that had done the damage; I wondered when he would just sit down and assess the injury. But John and my patient continued their conversation about pianos until it led John to the story of his time working as a piano mover, and the time he and his crew, on a misadventure with cables and pulleys, accidentally dropped an incredibly valuable grand piano from a fourth-floor window onto a Manhattan sidewalk. By the end of this story, both John and my patient were roaring with laughter.

The patient's anxiety and pain were soothed in that moment. John had established trust by showing that he, too, was a fallible person just trying his best to do right. I honestly don't even remember what we decided to do about the hematoma under the patient's toenail. That isn't the lesson that stuck with me over the twenty-plus years since that encounter. What left an indelible impression was the way a literal world leader in his field had taken the time to create a personal connection with a patient by sharing stories and laughter. If John had done that merely to ease the patient's pain and establish trust, that alone would have been admirable.

But I sensed that this wasn't John's main motivation. He did it because he enjoyed sharing a story and a laugh with someone; he sought out a moment at work to make a human connection and feed his own soul. He allowed himself to enjoy his work; he celebrated the privilege to heal that his job brought him. I took note of that moment, and even though I've left clinical medicine, it still influences me as a middle school teacher. In the same way that patients are more likely to follow the suggestions of a doctor with whom they connect, students learn best from teachers with whom they connect.

Going to school athletic events is a great way to figure out what our young people love to do. Cheering them on while they compete creates a substrate for conversations and connections. But for me, nothing beats a play or talent show to catch glimpses of students' personalities. I'll never forget watching one of the sixth-grade soccer players I coach march onto the stage of a full auditorium last spring, sit down at the piano, and belt out an Adele song that brought the house down. Now, when I see her in the hallway, I get to ask which songs she is working on for the next talent show, instead of focusing on nothing but her soccer training. If I get to teach her in eighth grade, thanks to a multifaceted connection, odds are good that she will be attentive and engaged in the classroom. That's a win-win for both student and teacher.

Despite his towering accomplishments, John maintained a powerful sense of humility. He was generous in describing the pitfalls he had suffered over the course of his career and didn't forget to mention the times when he wished he'd made different decisions. He'd seen hubris hurt and kill people, so he fiercely guarded against overconfidence in himself as well as those under his tutelage. Like John, the best leaders I've worked for all had a knack for recalling times when they were the least competent member of the team. The openness of those leaders made them disarming, approachable, and compassionate. Careerists and corporate climbers, on the other hand, are incapable of acknowledging that they were once incompetent neophytes. That segment of their lives, if they remember it at all, recalls a time of discomfort and humiliation. These people make abysmal leaders who are doomed to fail because they lack leadership's most essential trait: empathy.

In my chief resident year, I was working with John on the New Year's Eve overnight shift. It's worth pausing to mention that the department chairman and decorated leader of emergency medicine didn't have to work the New Year's Eve overnight shift in an urban ER. He was there because he didn't assign himself any more importance than his less-tenured peers; he worked New Year's that night because he had been off for Christmas, and each physician worked one or the other. The ER was as busy as you'd expect on New Year's Eve. John and I didn't get to talk much. By then, I'd earned enough of his trust to work about as independently as I was comfortable with. One of our more experienced nurses approached me around 2 a.m.

"Dr. Marx needs you to come help him in room three," she said quietly. "He's having trouble with a central line."

I had to pause for a moment as I thought, *This thirty-year veteran, this GOAT of emergency medicine, thinks I can place a central line that he can't?* I tried to fight the absurdity of the notion as I strode into room three. I glanced at John and his emaciated patient, then began to gather supplies so that I could assist or, heaven forbid, take over. "How can I help?" I was able to utter.

"Mr. Thompson"—a pseudonym for confidentiality's sake—"is massively dehydrated, and we can't get an IV or any other vascular access. He needs lots of fluids and antibiotics. He has HIV/AIDS and is significantly immune suppressed."

John continued gentle attempts to place a large-bore vascular access device (a central line, or fancy IV) into the patient's right subclavian vein (a typically large vein under the collar bone that leads directly back to the heart). He just wasn't connecting. When a patient is dehydrated, their veins literally shrink and flatten out, making them more difficult to find with a needle. I tried an internal pep talk: *Maybe a different doctor giving it a try will produce a different result,* I thought as I donned my mask, gown, and sterile gloves to assist. I stepped in beside John. As I did, I saw dark blood rush into the syringe he was holding; he had successfully hit the correct spot. It was smooth sailing from there, and I stepped away to break out of my sterile gear and find the next patient who most needed our help.

"Thanks, Keith," John called. "You must have brought the right aura."

I never thanked John for demonstrating his confidence in me. It was flattering, to be sure. But the moment he asked for my help was far too humbling for me to even bring it up. John died suddenly a few years after I had finished residency, and I never got to properly thank him for his confidence and leadership. But on the rare occasions that I manage to channel his humility, generosity, and humor, I like to think that I'm carrying his soul. Since John was an example for hundreds of emergency physicians, currently practicing and retired alike, we all share the honor of carrying his soul and multiplying his influence as we, in turn, mentor others.

Realizing our own competence is thrilling. Every resident and young doctor experiences this spark of joy. I bet almost all young professionals do. There was a phase of my career when performing emergency procedures for critical patients felt uplifting and fun; I was experiencing that thrill of competence. When patients were in trouble and required quick, decisive action and skill, I increasingly became the go-to person, the one they needed. Securing challenging airways, inserting fancy vascular access devices and chest tubes, and guiding dislocated bones back into place can transiently make someone feel like a superhero. The operative word here is *transiently.* Sadly, the thrill of competence wears off. At least, it did for me. The realization hit hard and all at once.

About ten years into my life in the ER, I was winding down a dizzying evening shift. Most ERs are busiest in the afternoon and evening: that portion of the twenty-four-hour cycle when the volume of new arrivals, hospital logjams, and staff shift changes converge to create a perfect storm of chaos, stagnation, and angst. When the doc who would replace me on the night shift walked in twenty minutes early, like he always did,

I felt the weight lift from my shoulders. If anyone ever decides to make ER-themed stained-glass windows, the newly arriving physician should have a golden halo around their head.

"Brent, you're a saint," I chirped.

"Tell it to my wife," he quipped through his trademark smirk.

Brent and I had attended medical school together, where we sang in the same acapella group. No, I'm not joking. We reunited in our professional careers, where we shared a lot less harmony and a lot more dark humor.

Now, Brent hadn't even set his travel coffee mug down before the EMS radio announced that they were bringing in a gunshot victim. The patient had wounds to his head and right side of his chest, a fast heart rate, and low blood pressure. Before he'd even arrived, we knew he was in shock due to either blood loss or a completely collapsed lung. Our hospital did not require the surgeon to stay overnight, but instead to come within thirty minutes of the arrival of a patient with major trauma.

"I'll jump in and help out until surgery gets here," I announced to Brent. "Just run the show and tell me what you need me to do."

"Sounds good. Thanks," he responded gratefully.

We made our way down to the trauma room to put on splash gowns and shoe covers. (By the time a trauma team has finished resuscitating a patient, the trauma bay can resemble the set of a horror movie.) Soon enough, a seventeen-year-old kid with wounds as described on the radio was wheeled in. By the look of his head wound and his poor responsiveness, his injuries would likely be fatal. Meanwhile, the wound on the right side of his chest was a couple of inches below the collar bone; that was the reason for his low blood pressure. We got to work, and Brent directed the resuscitation of the patient like the experienced professional he was. I performed the "trauma trifecta" of intubating the patient, placing a large-bore chest tube to drain blood and re-expand his lung, and inserting a central line. As mentioned before, a central line is a fancy IV that is almost the caliber of a milkshake straw. When it's placed correctly, it ends at the vena cava, just a couple of inches away from the heart itself. It's handy in a resuscitation because it allows the clinical team to pour fluids and blood into a patient who is in shock. All three procedures went smoothly, and the patient's blood pressure and heart rate improved substantially. Soon, the on-call surgeon arrived. He was an experienced and affable surgical oncologist who had spent many years in the army.

"Fellas, I'm a surgical oncologist. The only time I should ever get called to a trauma case is if someone gets stabbed in the tumor," he joked. We chuckled and got back to work stabilizing the patient as the surgeon hung up his white coat in the corner of the trauma bay. Humor is a nearly universal coping mechanism among healthcare workers. Without laughter, the amount of pain, grief, loss, and death would be overwhelming, and these jobs would be entirely untenable.

The team made plans to take the patient to the operating room to more definitively control his bleeding, but I knew that there would be no recovery from his head wound. This trip to the OR was to stabilize the patient in hopes of providing the time necessary for doctors to discuss organ donation with his family. That would be the only hope for anything positive to come from this tragedy.

Brent blessed me and sent me on my way. I shuffled out of the ER and to my car, feeling despondent. Suddenly, I realized that in an earlier stage of my career, I would have been skipping out of the hospital, riding the thrill of accomplishing so many emergency procedures in a matter of minutes. But there was no thrill this time, zero. All I could imagine was the patient's devastated family hearing the news that their son was never coming home. It was the first time I let myself acknowledge that maybe I needed to do something different for a living.

Chapter 14

THE SOUL TICKLE

The connections we make in the course of a life,
maybe that's what heaven is.
—Fred Rogers

It's the easiest way to stay in the game:
By helping the younger kids, they're gonna preach for you.
—George Clinton

A FEW MONTHS AFTER THE DISCOURAGING realization that I would probably never experience thrills or joy at work again, I had an encounter that, in retrospect, changed the course of my life. During another evening shift in the ER, I felt what I now call the *soul tickle*. To be fair, it is likely that I had felt it before then, but a specific encounter with a patient that night allowed me to make a clear connection. While working through a particularly challenging case, some combination of persistence, experience, good fortune, and doubt allowed me to finally arrive at a complex diagnosis. I called the hospitalist to arrange for the patient's admission and further treatment, then went and updated the patient with the news.

As I was leaving the room, she said, "I can't thank you enough for what you just did for me. I know it wasn't easy." She managed a chuckle. "Nothing about me is easy to figure out."

I walked back to my computer with a tingling sensation at the back of my neck, right at the base of my skull. It wasn't alarming, uncomfortable, or terribly intense; it was very pleasant and radiated up the back of my head and down into my neck. The feeling lasted for about ten or fifteen seconds, then it was gone. I made a mental note of it and kept working. Over the coming months and years, I noticed the feeling returning in similar situations. Every time a patient or family showed gratitude for my compassion and expertise, the same feeling would arrive at the base of my skull. The physiology of the feeling is mysterious to me, but I suspect it involves the sudden release of some combination of dopamine, serotonin, and oxytocin in specific areas of my brain. In a less scientific sense, I think that, in each instance, my soul became aware that it had served its purpose. I had discovered a truth and created a connection, and now someone who was suffering had gained a measure of comfort or relief. My soul was experiencing joy—it was smiling.

During some downtime at school while writing this book, I was chatting with Corley, our school's librarian, about this odd feeling. I listed the common threads of the situations that produced it and speculated about why it happens to me. Corley is a young mom who's bubbly, well read, and overall, pretty brilliant. She's a "jill-of-all-trades" who often serves as the glue that holds our middle school faculty together. She'll take on a class or two every semester, and she unfailingly and enthusiastically steps in to help when any of us are in a bind. "It sounds like you're describing ASMR," she offered after hearing my thoughts and stories.

"What's ASMR?" I responded.

"It stands for autonomous sensory meridian response. People can feel it in response to something they see or hear that's especially soothing or satisfying. It brings that tingle in the scalp, neck, and upper back that you described. The first time I remember getting it, I was in grade school watching a factory line video of crayons being made, lined up, labeled, and sorted. I think the incredible order and perfection of the process excited the pathway in my brain."

I remembered feeling something similar upon reaching the top of a mountain on a hike with my sister along the Appalachian Trail outside Roanoke, Virginia. Seeing the wide, nearly panoramic vista on a gorgeous late-September day, coupled with the feeling of achievement of reaching the top after a long climb, brought a mild but pleasant chill to my upper spine. Just today, while working out on a cardio machine, I was feeling mellow and listening to Crosby, Stills, Nash & Young. A similar feeling hit as their voices reached the harmonic crescendo of "Southern Cross." Likely, the feeling I describe as a soul tickle exists along the spectrum of what many people know as ASMR.[44] For me, one difference between the two is that the soul tickle carries an intensity that forces me to pause what I'm doing. I don't think I could continue exercising through it, for example. Additionally, the soul tickle only occurs when my own actions or efforts produce joy, relief, or gratitude in *someone else*.

A few months after the satisfying ER patient case I described earlier, the soul tickle hit me again. This time, an unexpected plot twist made it even more intense. I was on the day shift and had just left a patient room. I was headed back to my desk to enter orders and spotted a young man in jeans and a trucker cap waiting there for me. He was probably in his late twenties and looked vaguely familiar, but I couldn't quite recall where I had seen him before.

"Hey, Doc, I just wanted to come thank you for everything you did for my dad over there the other night," he said as he tilted his head toward room six and extended his hand for a shake. My heart sank into my stomach as I suddenly remembered the case.

About three nights earlier, EMS had hauled in a burly, bearded man in his mid-fifties a little after midnight on my overnight shift. He was complaining of chest and abdominal pain, and he was so sweaty, he looked like he'd just gotten out of the shower. Diaphoresis, or severe sweating of the face and torso that is out of proportion to the environment, is a sign that quickly gets the attention of everyone working in the ER. It typically means that a patient is pumping out adrenaline and its biochemical cousins just to stay alive. That mode of survival can only sustain someone for a short time before they collapse. The paramedic, Ann, handed me the patient's EKG. It was normal. Ann was one of the best paramedics I ever worked with. She was keen, compassionate, and never overconfident. She knew something serious was going on with her patient.

"We gave him aspirin, and I did another EKG because he *looks* like he's having a heart attack. See—he's sweating the monitor leads off!" she exclaimed while sticking a couple of the leads back onto the patient's skin.

"This EKG is normal as well," I remarked.

"I know. I need you to figure out what's wrong, because it's something bad," Ann pleaded.

I talked with the patient while I pulled up his electronic record. Our team got him attached to our monitors and found his heart rate and blood pressure to be normal. Considering the copious amount of adrenaline the patient was circulating, I had expected his blood pressure to be much higher. This surprise made me worry that the normal reading was falsely reassuring.

It's a pretty consistent phenomenon that ER staff members who work weekend overnight shifts are incredible. If you know people who work in the ER, ask them, and I bet they'll tell you the same thing. My team that night was loaded with all-stars. I stood back and got a bit more information from the patient while Paula and Angela went to work. In about three minutes, they had two huge IVs in place, a full panel of labs drawn, the patient's information entered into the computer system, and an EKG of our own. Again, the tracing was normal. I found no hospital, clinic, or ER records on our patient in the system.

"How long have you lived here, sir?" I asked.

His wife and son walked in as he was answering. "I was born and raised here. I've been here my whole life."

"I'm asking because we don't have any medical records on you in the system," I explained.

"Doc, I honestly don't remember the last time I went to see a doctor," he replied as he grimaced through the pain.

Looking terrified, his family scoldingly agreed. The ominous signs were adding up. It's really unlikely for a fifty-seven-year-old man who hasn't been to the doctor in twenty years to roll in at midnight pouring sweat and feeling chest pain due to indigestion. With the bedside ultrasound, I took a quick look for an aortic aneurysm, a problem that could kill our patient in a matter of minutes. I didn't see an obvious aneurysm, but bowel gas was obscuring the picture. Air is the enemy of ultrasound—bowel gas in the wrong place can render the images uninterpretable.

"We've got to go to CT. He needs to be the next one on the table." I hurried over to the CT suite and found the CT tech, Beth, finishing up with a study. "Beth, I've got a super sick gent who looks like he's about to die. I need a picture of every blood vessel from his chin to his thighs."

She immediately understood what I meant. "Contrasted CT of the chest, abdomen, and pelvis—got it. Hustle him on over. I'll bump the next case on my schedule."

"Awesome. We'll be right back."

Our team wheeled the patient over to the scanner and transferred him to the table. Whenever I was really worried about someone who needed a CT, I'd travel with them in case they suddenly deteriorated while they were over there. Plus, I'd get to see the images as soon as they were acquired. Our patient's aortic arch immediately caught my eye as Beth scrolled through the first images.

"Sweet Georgia Brown, he's got a raging aortic dissection!"

An aortic dissection is a tear in the wall of the aorta, the main artery leaving the heart. It has about the same diameter as a garden hose. The tear in the aortic wall creates a false lumen, a new but highly ineffective path for blood to collect within. Unlike an aneurysm, a dissection typically doesn't burst open. Instead, the false passage can block off arteries downstream. If a dissection in the aortic arch isn't fixed quickly, it can lead to strokes, heart attacks, kidney damage, and other major problems.

I called our on-call thoracic and vascular surgeon, a soft-spoken, thorough, and talented guy who was just a couple of years older than me. He showed up almost immediately to meet the patient and made plans to get him to the operating room.

"How do you think he'll do?" I wondered.

"It's going to be tough. His aorta is tearing stem to stern. It's a huge challenge to even get a patient with a dissection this severe on the bypass machine. It's really easy to put a tube into the false lumen instead of the true one," he responded.

A cardiopulmonary bypass involves inserting appropriately sized hoses into large blood vessels adjacent to the heart. While on bypass, the patient's blood instead circulates through a machine that adds oxygen and removes waste products; the bypass machine temporarily takes over the job of the patient's heart and lungs. Thanks to this procedure, the patient's heart can literally be stopped and held still while surgeons do their work. Since hitting a stationary target is much easier than hitting a moving one, many heart surgeries require patients to first be placed on bypass. That way, the surgical team can do good instead of harm. As the surgeon had said, my patient with a dissection in his aortic arch would need a cardiopulmonary bypass for the operation to be successful.

Soon enough, the patient was wheeled away to the operating room. I wasn't optimistic, but there was no time to chant lamentations. Four new patients had arrived while I was occupied with the prior case. I picked up the next chart and got back to work.

That background should help explain why my heart sank when the patient's somber-looking son came to meet me a few days later. I was guessing that his dad hadn't pulled through.

"Yes, of course I remember! How is he doing?" I asked, then immediately wished I could shovel the words right back into my mouth. *Why didn't I just say, "I'm so sorry"?* I thought as I mentally kicked myself.

"Oh, he's doing great! He's up walking the halls, and the doctors say he can probably come home tomorrow," he cheerily replied. "I can't thank you and the nurses enough for how quick you got him figured out. We were so worried."

This time, the feeling at the back of my neck and skull hit immediately and more explosively than the first time I noticed it. I figured this was because I had been expecting terrible news and had instead received a huge dose of validation. The patient's son and I shared a handshake and a one-armed "bro hug" before he turned and walked out of the ER doors and toward the main hospital. I couldn't wait to see the weekend night team again to tell them the news.

I've taken a few informal polls of teacher coworkers to see if the sensation I'm describing happens to anyone else. About a quarter or a third of them seem to relate a similar experience. I'm not sure if some people cannot feel it, or if they just haven't yet been able to fully plug into experiences that provoke it. Over the past two years, I've realized that I haven't lost the feeling forever just because I've changed careers. I can feel the same feeling teaching young people. Let me set the backdrop before I tell you how I learned that I can still feel the soul tickle, even outside of medicine.

When I signed on to teach eighth-grade science just over two years ago, my previous job experience helped me feel instantly comfortable with one semester of the curriculum, the one on human body systems. The second semester of electricity and circuits was much more daunting. Twenty-five years had passed since my two semesters of college physics. I hadn't thought about current, resistance, or how batteries work in a quarter century. I needed to relearn all of that and more. Now, I love to learn, but in that situation, my healthy dose of impostor syndrome saved me. I can't think of many things that compel preparation more than impostor syndrome does; I am never able to forgive myself when I'm exposed as an incompetent failure.

So over the summer before my first year of full-time teaching, I got to work and gave myself a crash course on electricity and circuits. I bought a physics textbook with problems in it, read the pertinent chapters, and solved all the problems—twice. I watched videos illustrating the key concepts. I went into the classroom alone and performed all the labs by myself. I worked through all the worksheets, quizzes, and tests I could find in the curriculum. Don't take this to mean that I felt prepared on the first day of second semester—I didn't. A medical intern year and the first year as a teacher have a striking number of parallels; having never taught the material before, I walked into every day unsure if I would sink or swim.

My eighth-grade science counterpart, Bonnie, proved to be a godsend for me. She kept me organized, showed me how to manage the clerical work of teaching, and brought the experience and skill of an army quartermaster to lab preparation and function. I can't think of anyone in my professional past who wanted me to succeed more than she did during my first year of teaching.

The first weeks of the semester passed with fewer hiccups than I had expected, and I was beginning to feel cautiously optimistic. But sometime in late February, the conceptual difficulty of the curriculum began to increase, and I could tell the kids were struggling with it. I started to question my capability again.

During one help session in March, Peyton, a gregarious and typically optimistic student plodded in. "Dr. Pochick, I just can't understand how adding a bulb in parallel *decreases* a circuit's resistance. A bulb is a resistor. How can adding a resistor *decrease* resistance in a circuit?"

I tried using the analogy of the cafeteria checkout line, which invites a mental image of only one cashier ringing people out on a popular lunch day, like when the dining hall is slinging out popcorn chicken. When the student gets the idea that thirty or forty kids will be in that single line, and they'll all have to wait for what seems like forever, I get them to imagine what changes when two more lines open. The flow through checkout will increase, of course, which happens because the new paths decrease the resistance of the flow through checkout. Even though there is a resistor (another cashier sitting at a checkout register) in each of the parallel paths added, the overall resistance decreases thanks to the new paths. This seemed to partially land with Peyton, but I could tell that he wasn't completely intellectually satisfied.

"Let's build a model and figure this out, Peyton," I offered, beginning to set up a simple circuit with two bulbs in parallel. I instructed Peyton to place a compass under the wire attached to the positive terminal of the battery. We had already learned that a compass can gauge the amount of charge flow through a wire. "What's the compass reading right now?" I asked as only one of the two bulbs was looped into the circuit, meaning there was only one path for charge to flow through.

"Twenty degrees clockwise," he replied.

"Now, let's add another resistor in a *new* path, a path parallel to the first bulb." I made the connection, and both bulbs lit equally. "What's the reading now?"

"Thirty-five degrees clockwise," Peyton answered.

I offered a leading question: "So adding the new parallel path did what to the charge flow out of the battery?"

"It increased it. The compass deflected more," came the reply.

"So charge flow went up when we added the parallel path. Did it go up because we increased the voltage? Did we add more batteries to push and pull harder?"

"No. The battery stayed the same," he responded.

"So if charge flow through the battery increased when we added the parallel path, and we didn't change the voltage at all, what did adding the parallel path accomplish?" I asked while eyeing the formula for Ohm's law on the whiteboard.

His eyes followed mine, then lit up. "Adding the parallel path decreased the overall resistance. It's why the charge flow increased!"

Upon his realization, the base of my skull and back of my neck tingled in a familiar way. The soul tickle identical to the one I used to feel working in medicine had returned. It turns out that facilitating someone else's recognition of truth tickles my soul too. I've allowed myself to become increasingly attuned to this feeling at school—to pause, recognize, and appreciate it. It's become a powerful reminder of why I do what I do. It marks the fulfillment of my purpose.

About three years ago, after considerable hesitation, I agreed to coach my younger daughter's recreational league soccer team. Soccer was not a sport I'd played much growing up, and I was sure that within a half hour of the first practice, my lack of experience would expose me as an impostor. But none of the other parents wanted to be head coach, and the girls really wanted to play, so I signed on to lead them. From the first minute, the kids truly enjoyed themselves on the field, and practices felt more like recess than regimented training sessions. It turned out that I could pretty easily fool fourth graders into believing that I knew what I was doing. We weren't very good at first; we lost a lot more games than we won. At least once during that initial season, we got smoked so badly that mercy rule stipulations went into effect. But it wasn't long before soccer practice night became my favorite night of the week. The girls hustled, laughed, and encouraged each other. Being a part of the group and watching the girls connect brought me joy.

In the beginning, creating a culture of trust and safety in practice and on the sidelines was vitally important to me. My experience as a young athlete participating in team sports taught me that a culture like this is not a given. Each time I look back upon the amount of bullying I watched, endured, and sometimes participated in while playing middle and high school sports, I find it increasingly unsettling. When I was a scrawny fourteen-year-old rising freshman at stay-away football camp, a group of us was walking back to the dorms after lunch to get ready for the afternoon practice. A senior on my own high school team who outweighed me by almost 150 pounds started repeatedly shoving me and calling me "bitch." I acquiesced and tolerated it. What was I going to do in a fistfight with a 285-pound defensive tackle? Occurrences like this were ubiquitous; hazing was viewed as nothing more than an unpleasant aspect of an otherwise positive high school football package. Years later, I understand that leading a culture of people who tolerate bullying of its smaller and weaker members is functionally equivalent to enabling and empowering the bullies themselves. Discussions with friends and colleagues who grew up elsewhere have illustrated that a toxic culture in team sports was pervasive; now, more than twenty-five years later, tales of sports hazing seem just as common as they were back then.

Experiences like the one I described above, combined with my lack of athletic talent, galvanized my desire to earn respect as a football player. Since I wasn't one of the kids who saw his name in the paper very often, I had to make my mark in other ways. As a sophomore, I remember lining up for a second-half kickoff on a bitterly cold November night. I spotted a hulking lineman across from me on the receiving team. I imagined that he was one of the abusive bullies on his own team and decided that I was about to earn the respect my own leaders denied me. If you ever played organized football, you know how the kickoff grants a huge advantage to the kicking team's players over the receiving team's blockers. As soon as the ball was launched from its tee, I drew a bead on this ogre and hit a full sprint as he shuffled backward. A couple of seconds later, he turned to find a human guided missile striking his sternum as my leading right shoulder made contact. We tumbled over each other a couple times on the frozen ground. Someone else on my team thankfully made the tackle, because I had no interest whatsoever in finding the kick returner. As I regained my feet, I found our sideline erupting, coaches and teammates each hollering and spewing clouds of frozen water vapor into the Appalachian sky. I had just felled a giant. When I reached the sideline, an excited teammate jumped on me and told me that my hit sounded like a rifle shot echoing through the hills. A triple dose of dopamine was released in my brain as I instantly realized how I'd leave my mark as a football player. While I'd never be the one scoring touchdowns or winning all-state honors, I could earn an opponent's respect.

As a middle school teacher, and especially as a youth sports coach, I try to create a culture quite different than the one in which I grew up. Thankfully, and with a lot of help, our soccer team has accomplished this. Our girls just finished their seventh season together, and this time we went undefeated and won the league championship. These are the same kids who were getting trounced in their rookie campaign. I've had some time to think about the factors that allowed them to come so far so quickly, and I'm humbly aware that coaching isn't what turned them into the top U14 team in the league. First of all, we've had incredible continuity from season to season. Since we show up at the first practice of each season already knowing one another's names, strengths, preferences, and weaknesses, we can pick up exactly where we left off. We can immediately start honing skills and strategy, instead of burning the first three practices getting to know one another. Furthermore, not once in seven seasons have I received an angry or critical comment from a parent. In the modern world of youth sports, it seems unheard of that not a single parent has called, texted, or emailed me about how much or which position their daughter is playing. Instead of criticism from the parents, I've gotten help. Two other dads join us for practice and on the sidelines during games.

This environment enabled the girls to trust one another early on. They learned from the adults on the pitch, and from one another, that failing doesn't bring shame or ridicule; it brings understanding and encouragement from their coaches and teammates. So the girls aren't afraid to fail. That's a key ingredient to success in any pursuit. A fear of failure prevents any athlete from competing at their full potential. When our team began playing without fearing failure, they became a potent force and a joy to watch. A trusting team that feels safe and supported can, and often does, defeat a more talented team. Chemistry really matters, especially with younger athletes. Without a feeling of trust and safety, it's impossible for young athletes to enjoy the new activity. When youth players do not sense trust and safety, they learn less, develop less confidence, and experience anxiety instead of enjoyment.

Sometimes, when I'm feeling self-important, I like to imagine our players as reflections of myself as a young athlete—talentless grinders who are out to earn respect. While we do have our share of gritty hustlers on the roster, we are much more than that. The skill, finesse, speed, and power our girls have developed in spite of me is pretty humbling. Watching those fierce young women compete as athletes and grow as people tickles my soul. I began coaching youth soccer about a year before I made the career transition into education, and the joy I found with those kids on the pitch undoubtedly brought me the measure of certainty I needed to confidently make the career jump into guiding young people for a living.

As a scientist, I've tried to teach myself to examine how things happen before delving into why they do. Like I mentioned previously, I don't think the universe needs a purpose to exist. With that in mind, I'm uncertain about whether there is a greater purpose or meaning in the feeling I've described. But I do know that I want it to happen more often. At a bare minimum, the soul tickle is a psychological reward for pursuing truth and connecting with others. The mere realization that seeking truth and helping others can feel physically rewarding is a testament to the beauty of both the human body and humanity itself.

The roots of America's burgeoning mental health crisis are legion. I believe that crushing loneliness and the toxic side effects of our ceaseless drive to achieve are the main culprits. Upon the backdrop of our society's mental health epidemic, our culture has become justifiably obsessed with "self-care." Our more open attitudes toward discussing mental health and mental illness are undeniable steps in the right direction. It's restorative to take an afternoon nap, get a massage, or eat a slice of cheesecake. It could be, however, that we tend to overlook a couple of the simplest means of self-care. It turns out that seeking truth and improving the life of someone else can be self-care too. They are two ways we can tickle our own souls. Discover the situations and activities that tickle your soul, then unapologetically seek them out. You deserve them.

EPILOGUE

As I STARE DOWN THE finish line of this effort, I am also exploring the first steps of publishing it. It may have taken nearly fifty years, but I finally achieved the patience and drive necessary to reach what, for me, was an incredibly ambitious creative goal. With that in mind, I can confidently say that this book is a testament to my own personal growth. I'm someone who generally has lots of ideas but struggles mightily with putting them into action or seeing them to completion. The drudgery of muscling through the creation of a references page, for example, is something the younger me would have found intolerable. Our personalities and identities may tend to hold fairly firm throughout our lives, but they aren't absolutely static. This book serves as proof of that fact, and that promise alone brings me a measure of hope.

Thankfully, I don't have any delusions of grandeur about selling millions of books, winning awards, or starting a new religion. Odds are fair that the book doesn't sell at all, and instead I'll have a couple dozen hardcover prints made and give them to family and friends to fill out sparse bookcases and use as coasters. Even if that's all that comes from publishing this book, I'll be satisfied that I've left behind a unique time capsule for my kids. I've been without my mom for over twenty-five years now, and while dozens of different memories of her can surface at varied, sometimes inexplicable times, most of the physical evidence she left behind is now gone. Maybe this book will serve as a tangible touchstone for my kids when they get older. Maybe they'll pick it up one day twenty years from now when they're facing a difficult choice, and my words will give them pause to consider their own identities. Even if nothing else comes of it, my children can hold this book and open it after I'm long gone, and it will refresh their memories of me.

WHAT DO I HOPE READERS of this book take away from it? I hope I have brought you a new or renewed realization that inertia, not death, is the enemy of life. By extension, I hope I have shown you that the toxic pitfalls of cynicism and nihilism represent inertia of the soul. I want you to understand that the only people who've ever brought positive change to the world are people who believed that they could. Once someone stops believing in their own potential to build a better future, they've conceded to inertia, even though they're still biologically alive. We should never settle for the cultural inertia of the status quo; we should unceasingly and unapologetically search for ways to discover new truths and lift humanity up. By definition, an eternal cause can never be fully won; our work and the struggle must carry on. To settle is to cede victory to inertia.

I will be satisfied if just a handful of readers choose to reject nihilism and instead adopt or recommit to an eternal cause. I also hope you have also gained a greater appreciation for the healthiness of doubting what you've read or been taught. No book, website, or person is an infallible source of truth. Hopefully, some readers will embrace the understanding that a solid, oft-examined identity serves as a map to finding your purpose. If just one reader ignites their own willpower so that they begin to approach decision-making with greater levels of consciousness and introspection, I will be thrilled. Maybe they can use that newfound agency to face down an addiction or cement a healthy habit. Additionally, I'm optimistic that my readers will come to further appreciate their own inner fortitude, and realize that strength and power over others, if they are related at all, are only distant cousins. Maybe a couple of readers will realize that it's natural to feel incompetent when trying a new activity, and they'll adopt an approach of curiosity and humility while they're gaining confidence in a new field.

Finally, I hope that at least a few readers begin to approach seeking truth and serving others with more than an attitude of duty. If we let them, these pursuits can bring us so much more fulfillment than the mere satisfaction of checking boxes off our list of human responsibilities. Ultimately, I hope I've helped spark the realization that seeking truth and reliably and repeatedly lifting up the people who need us brings joy to our souls and greater meaning to our lives.

ACKNOWLEDGMENTS

CREATING A LIST OF PEOPLE to thank after a project like this is almost as tall a task as writing the book itself. Every family member, teacher, role model, patient, coworker, and student who influenced me, whether positively or negatively, rightfully deserves some credit. Like every human, my worldview and philosophy were shaped by innumerable people and experiences. Since I can't possibly list them all, I want to focus on the people who supported me through the process of writing and editing the manuscript, as well as those who advised and guided me through a largely uncharted career transition.

My wife Meredith will be the first person to confess that a spouse's professional transition creates a legion of stressful scenarios and discussions. But every time I called uncertainty or angst down upon our family, she responded with generosity and understanding. The schedule of a family with young kids is a house of cards—every time a piece gets plucked away and moved to a new location, the entire structure is at risk of collapse. Previously stable travel plans, budgeting, savings, and all other priorities become suddenly negotiable. My wife hasn't just tolerated the instability and chaos—she has patiently and expertly managed them.

Our first daughter Taylor is an academic powerhouse, an accomplished dancer, and a loyal friend; she is the kind of self-motivated kid that every parent dreams of having. Nothing I've done in my life justifies the grace I was afforded when she arrived to truly set our family's course into motion. Kaycie, our youngest daughter, has a unique gift for bringing a goofy, high-energy fervor to every activity. Games, cooking, sports, flights, and even studying become rollicking escapades just because she's there—Kaycie greets every day with infectious joy. Her unique blend of humor, kindness, athletic talent, and work ethic never fails to humble me.

My dad and sisters played enormous roles in instilling the values and beliefs I articulate in this book. While my dad and I have never seen eye-to-eye on everything, he always encouraged my curiosity and helped pull me through a challenging stretch of my young life. For years, he worked to keep me clothed and fed, and he saved enough money to put my sister and me through college.

Not many American kids had to grow up as fast as my sister Kristi did. At age six, she welcomed both a baby brother and sister into her life. Despite the added duties of serving as a backup parent, she confidently blazed a successful trail for my twin sister and me to follow. Kristi graciously and patiently offered probing questions and editing suggestions in the early stages of crafting this book. Over forty-eight years, my twin Kathy and I have never lived more than a few miles apart. While our details differ somewhat, we've been on the same timeline through every phase of our lives since before the day we were born. Kathy is an "old soul" who has never met a stranger in her life. Both of my sisters share a love of people and laughter that make them the focal point of fun for almost every gathering.

Anyone who spends twenty years in clinical medicine is guaranteed to come across a brilliant, witty, and driven cast of characters; I surely did. Medical school classmates share a unique bond. The long road to earning professional respect and esteem is filled with humbling episodes of serving as the least valuable member of a new team each month. Humor is a useful defense mechanism; we employed it as often as we could. Dr. Milan Nadkarni quickly became a physician I worked to emulate as he confidently served families in the Pediatric ER at Wake Forest; he played a pivotal role in my selection of emergency medicine as a career.

Compared to medical school, residency brings longer hours and a near vertical stretch of the learning curve; the responsibilities are far greater and the decisions are much more consequential. Residency is where one becomes the doctor they'll be for decades to come. The clinical faculty members of Emergency Medicine at Carolinas Medical Center in the early 2000s were living examples of the dedication and tenacity my fellow residents and I needed to expertly evaluate and care for the thousands of ill, injured, and anxious who'd walk, limp, or roll through our doors over the course of our professional lives. My residency director Parker Hays modeled the ultimate combination of competence, confidence, and self-doubt that dozens of us still aim to attain and pass on to the young people under our tutelage. Patrick O'Malley is a former residency mate and current good friend who understands the internal struggle of an emergency physician considering a dramatic career change. The "sunk costs" that result from years of sacrifice and training, as well as the nagging sense of letting people down, function to paralyze and prevent action. This paralysis brings the angst of professional and personal inertia. I distinctly remember the conversation Patrick and I had on an October day while paddleboarding on a South Carolina lake; although our homes were a hundred miles apart, psychologically, we were living in the same place. After that conversation, I allowed myself "permission" to leave medicine and march into the metaphorical wilderness of education. Kevin Smallman and I were both grizzled veterans of the ER when we became coworkers a couple of years before the COVID pandemic flipped the healthcare world upside down. The tales of absurdity, memes, and fart jokes we shared sustained us both when we were running on empty.

From the day I picked up my first substitute teaching shift during a particularly rough COVID wave in 2021, my coworkers at Providence Day School made me feel included. As a new teacher with minimal experience in education, I often needed guidance in lesson planning and navigating disciplinary dilemmas; as a product of the analog '80s, I plodded through digital curricula and online grading at a snail's pace. Despite these challenges in the early months of my transition, I never once felt lost at sea—there were always dozens of experienced teachers who would go out of their way to help me. And when I needed some room to try something new in the classroom, I was afforded the autonomy to occasionally fall on my face and learn from the experience. Special thanks go out to my fellow middle school science teachers—I mentioned Bonnie Wright, our department head, in the pages of the book. I've never come across anyone in my professional life who was as invested in my success as Bonnie is. Doug Burgess spent hours patiently teaching me the physics of optics when I got my first bullpen call to cover seventh grade science classes for a few months. Kelly Gordon has never forgotten what it was like being a first-year teacher; she still graciously shares lab ideas and strategies for prioritizing tasks. With humor and generosity, Andrea Villegas unselfishly stepped into a less comfortable role in order to welcome me onboard and balance our faculty's skills and experience. I gained a much-needed boost of confidence to make the leap of faith and change careers when I watched James Chamberlain pull it off a couple of years ahead of me. Our middle school head, Lee Tappy, took a chance on an unproven forty-five-year-old who was anything but a sure bet. His confidence in me and assurances over those initial months were worth far more than he'll ever realize. Alyssa Schumacher in the middle school administrative office is still an unfailingly welcoming presence, just like she was the first day I showed up.

Camryn Lozier, the book's cover artist, is one of the students I taught "wire-to-wire" in my first year as a middle school science teacher. Her artistic vision and talent became evident early that year as she gladly took on the artist's role for group projects and produced eye-catching impromptu doodles during class. In the opening stage of my new career, Camryn demonstrated the powerful and humbling truth that each middle-school student brings a unique collection of interests and talents to our classroom every day.

In sharing her personal experience with addiction, my cousin Sarah Holland generously lent vulnerability to my chapter on willpower. Her approachability and grace are proof of her spirit and desire to help those who need a reminder that tragedy can bring triumph.

When our second daughter Kaycie was a few months old, my wife and I met Gloria Baker. She was working in the childcare area of the fitness club where we went regularly to work out. It didn't take long for us to realize that we had stumbled upon a rare gem. Gloria came to care for the kids at least two or three times per week so that my wife and I could continue working full time. She shuttled them to school and preschool, got them to dance and gymnastics classes, and hauled them to libraries for kids' playtime events. In treating our daughters like they were her own, Gloria became a member of our little family. Even though she is older than my wife and me, Gloria's spirit is forever young. Only now, a few years into teaching middle school, do I fully appreciate her wisdom when she told me that being around young people can keep anyone young at heart.

Twenty-some years ago, I met my friend Walker Miller. One of my first memories of hanging out with him is when he organized a game of pickup tackle football in the parking lot of a Virginia Tech/East Carolina game here in Charlotte. About a half dozen of us limped into the stadium for the noon kickoff with fresh bruises and bloody road rash on our knees and elbows. Although we've grown up considerably since then, Walker still brings an infectious enthusiasm to any gathering. Our kids are the same age, and we've experienced the highs and lows of fatherhood in this city on the same chronology while looking at the same map. Like me, he gets genuinely excited to charge into the philosophical jungle and explore. The lure of its hidden treasures always overcomes our fear of the pitfalls as we hack through the underbrush to uncover a single tantalizing rabbit hole. Many of the past discussions Walker and I had provided fuel for this book. I've never had another friend like him.

There aren't enough words to thank the team of professionals at Warren Publishing. When my raw first draft arrived in the Warren inbox, Publisher Mindy Kuhn miraculously saw enough promise to give it the green light. My content editor Amy Klein teased at least two dozen personal stories and anecdotes out of me to nearly double the length of the original manuscript. Copyeditor Melisa Graham patiently and dutifully waded through a swamp of grammatical, punctuation, and formatting errors that only a B English student from Appalachia like me could create. Chief Editor Amy Ashby's encouraging, optimistic spirit and boundless flexibility provided a perfect balance of focus and freedom to accomplish what, for me, was a Herculean task. I'm immensely grateful for the entire team at Warren.

Finally, I'd like to thank the Unitarian Universalist Community of Charlotte. Perhaps more than anything else, each human's life is a spiritual journey of discovering one's place in the universe. Although I'm still new to the Universalist Community, I am confident that I was a Universalist before I knew such a thing existed. Rather than ignoring or even criticizing the ideology of other faiths, Universalists have a free-thinking and open-minded gentleness that encourages appreciation for kernels of truth, regardless of when or where they were found. Universalism is a truly liberating approach to the world and its problems that fosters personal growth and a humanity-centered moral clarity.

Humanity's causes are eternal. And so, our shared journey continues.

NOTES

1. Yunus A. Çengel, "Eighteen distinctive characteristics of life," *Heliyon* 9, no. 3, e13603 (2023), doi:10.1016/j.heliyon.2023.e13603.
2. *Britannica*, "Mule," last updated December 23, 2024, https://www.britannica.com/animal/mule-mammal.
3. Pedro Romero et al., "Computational prediction of human metabolic pathways from the complete human genome," *Genome Biology* 6, R2 (2005). https://doi:10.1186/gb-2004-6-1-r2.
4. Valerie Hedges, "Spinal Reflexes," in *Introduction to Neuroscience,* open edition. With content contributed by Casey Henley. Michigan State University Libraries, 2022, openbooks.lib.msu.edu/introneuroscience1/chapter/spinal-reflexes/.
5. Manabu Hori et al., "RNA interference reveals the escape response mechanism of *Paramecium* to mechanical stimulation," *Biophysics and Physicobiology* 20, no. 2, e200025 (2023), https://doi:10.2142/biophysico.bppb-v20.0025.
6. *Britannica*, "Inertia," last updated January 16, 2025, https://www.britannica.com/science/inertia.
7. Sabrina Libretti and Yana Puckett, "Physiology, Homeostasis," *StatPearls* [Internet], StatPearls Publishing, last updated May 1, 2023, https://www.ncbi.nlm.nih.gov/books/NBK559138/.
8. Tim Jankowiak, "Immanuel Kant," in the *Internet Encyclopedia of Philosophy*, accessed February 2, 2025, https://iep.utm.edu/kantview/.
9. Robin Materese and Ben P. Stein, editors, "Second: Introduction," SI Redefinition, National Institute of Standards and Technology, updated September 25, 2023, www.nist.gov/si-redefinition/second-introduction.
10. Yann Martel, *Life of Pi* (Knopf, 2001).
11. *Britannica*, "First Council of Nicaea," last updated March 29, 2024, https://www.britannica.com/event/First-Council-of-Nicaea-325.
12. Wyatt Massey, "The Protestant Bible and Catholic Bible are not the same book," *Chattanooga Times Free Press*, November 11, 2019, www.timesfreepress.com/news/2019/nov/08/protestant-bible-catholic-bible/.
13. *Britannica*, "Arius," last updated February 13, 2024, https://www.britannica.com/biography/Arius.
14. Ward H. Lamon, *The Life of Abraham Lincoln* (James R. Osgood and Company, 1872), Project Gutenberg, www.gutenberg.org/files/40977/40977-h/40977-h.htm.
15. Steven Nadler, "Baruch Spinoza," in *Stanford Encyclopedia of Philosophy* (Spring 2024 Edition) ed., Edward N. Zalta & Uri Nodelman, https://plato.stanford.edu/archives/spr2024/entries/spinoza/.
16. "Mahatma Gandhi Says He Believes In Christ But Not Christianity," *The Harvard Crimson,* January 11, 1927, www.thecrimson.com/article/1927/1/11/mahatma-gandhi-says-he-believes-in/.
17. "Antoine-Laurent Lavoisier," Science History Institute Museum and Library, accessed August 14, 2024, www.sciencehistory.org/education/scientific-biographies/antoine-laurent-lavoisier/.

18 "First Direct Evidence of Cosmic Inflation," Newsdesk, Smithsonian, posted March, 17 2014, www.si.edu/newsdesk/releases/first-direct-evidence-cosmic-inflation.

19 "Lincoln's Legacy: The Eloquent President," United States National Park Service, www.nps.gov/foth/lincoln-s-legacy-the-eloquent-president.htm.

20 B. Alberts, et al., "Chromosomal DNA and Its Packaging in the Chromatin Fiber," in *Molecular Biology of the Cell,* 4th ed. (Garland Science, 2002), available from https://www.ncbi.nlm.nih.gov/books/NBK26834/.

21 Kimberly A. McBennett et al., "Increasing life expectancy in cystic fibrosis: Advances and challenges," *Pediatric Pulmonology* 57 Suppl 1, Suppl 1 (2022): S5-S12, https://doi:10.1002/ppul.25733.

22 Sophie Lanzkron et al., "Mortality rates and age at death from sickle cell disease: U.S., 1979-2005," *Public Health Reports (Washington, D.C.: 1974)* 128, no. 2 (2013): 110-6, https://doi:10.1177/003335491312800206.

23 "2 Month - 5 Early Relational Health Developmental Milestone Timeline," Patient Care, American Academy of Pediatrics, www.aap.org/en/patient-care/early-childhood/milestone-timeline/.

24 *Britannica*, "Christian Reformed Church in North America," last updated December 3, 2023, https://www.britannica.com/topic/Christian-Reformed-Church-in-North-America.

25 Darryl Hart, "Calvinism in the United States," *Oxford Research Encyclopedia of American History*, posted June 9, 2016, accessed June 18, 2024, https://oxfordre.com/americanhistory/view/10.1093/acrefore/9780199329175.001.0001/acrefore-9780199329175-e-318.

26 "Religion in India: Tolerance and Segregation," Pew Research Center, June 19, 2021, www.pewresearch.org/religion/2021/06/29/attitudes-about-caste.

27 Mirosława Cichorek et al., "Skin melanocytes: biology and development," *Postepy Dermatologii i Alergologii* 30, no. 1 (2013): 30-41, https://doi:10.5114/pdia.2013.33376.

28 Oliver Burkeman, "The clockwork universe: is free will an illusion?" *The Guardian*, April 27, 2021, www.theguardian.com/news/2021/apr/27/the-clockwork-universe-is-free-will-an-illusion.

29 Joan Walsh Anglund, *A Cup of Sun: A Book of Poems* (Harcourt, Brace & World, 1967), 15.

30 Douglas T. Kenrick et al., "Renovating the Pyramid of Needs: Contemporary Extensions Built Upon Ancient Foundations," *Perspectives on Psychological Science: A Journal of the Association for Psychological Science* 5, no. 3 (2010): 292-314, https://doi:10.1177/1745691610369469.

31 Benno Artmann, "Euclidean geometry," *Britannica*, last updated May 16, 2024, https://www.britannica.com/science/Euclidean-geometry.

32 *Einstein's Big Idea*, written by David Bodanis, directed by Gary Johnstone, aired October 11, 2005, on PBS, NOVA: Full-Length Broadcast Collection, wtvi.pbslearningmedia.org/resource/nvfb-sci-einsteinsidea/wgbh-nova-einsteins-big-idea-full-length-broadcast/.

33 Carl W. Buehner, quoted in Richard L. Evans, *Richard Evans' Quote Book* (Publishers Press, 1971), 244.

34 "Did St. Francis Write the 'Prayer of St. Francis?'" St. Catherine of Siena Roman Catholic Church, accessed June 18, 2024, www.stcatherinercc.org/single-post/2017/09/27/did-st-francis-write-the-prayer-of-st-francis.

35 Tom Henderson, "Definition and Mathematics of Work," *Work and Energy,* The Physics Classroom, accessed on October 15, 2024, https://www.physicsclassroom.com.

36 Norizan Mohd Nurazzi et al., "15 - Natural nanofiller-based polymer composites in packaging applications," in *Synthetic and Natural Nanofillers in Polymer Composites* from the Woodhead Publishing Series in Composites Science and Engineering, ed. N.M. Nurazzi, R.A. Ilyas, S.M. Sapuan, A. Khalina (Woodhead Publishing, 2023), 331-348, https://doi.org/10.1016/B978-0-443-19053-7.00003-2.

37 Daisy Dobrijevic and Nola Taylor Tillman, "Black holes: Everything you need to know," Space, last updated May 19, 2023, www.space.com/15421-black-holes-facts-formation-discovery-sdcmp.html.

38 "The Washington Post's new motto predates Trump's election," Associated Press, Feb. 24, 2017, apnews.com/general-news-873b142df48c495485f7a6a1eaff021f.

39 Nienke C. Jonker et al., "The reward and punishment responsivity and motivation questionnaire (RPRM-Q): A stimulus-independent self-report measure of reward and punishment sensitivity that differentiates between responsivity and motivation," *Frontiers in Psychology* 13, (August 9, 2022), https://doi:10.3389/fpsyg.2022.929255.

40 Robert G. Lewis et al., "The Brain's Reward System in Health and Disease," *Advances in Experimental Medicine and Biology* 1344 (2021): 57-69, https://doi:10.1007/978-3-030-81147-1_4.

41 Philip Jean-Richard-Dit-Bressel et al., "Behavioral and neurobiological mechanisms of punishment: implications for psychiatric disorders," *Neuropsychopharmacology: Official Publication of the American College of Neuropsychopharmacology* 43, no. 8 (2018): 1639-1650, https://doi:10.1038/s41386-018-0047-3.

42 "What you need to know about willpower: The psychological science of self-control," American Psychological Association, accessed October 27, 2024, https://www.apa.org/topics/personality/willpower.

43 Eric C. Gaze, "Debunking the Dunning-Kruger effect—the least skilled people know how much they don't know, but everyone thinks they are better than average," *The Conversation*, May 8, 2023, https://theconversation.com/debunking-the-dunning-kruger-effect-the-least-skilled-people-know-how-much-they-dont-know-but-everyone-thinks-they-are-better-than-average-195527.

44 James V. Lloyd, Thomas P.O. Ashdown, and Lucy R. Jawad LR, "Autonomous Sensory Meridian Response: What is It? and Why Should We Care?" *Indian Journal of Psychological Medicine* 39, no 2. (Mar-Apr 2017):214-215. https://doi: 10.4103/0253-7176.203116.

www.ingramcontent.com/pod-product-compliance
Lightning Source LLC
Chambersburg PA
CBHW022012090426
42741CB00007B/1005